THE ILLUSTRATED ENCYCLOPEDIA OF

Buddhist Wisdom

THE ILLUSTRATED ENCYCLOPEDIA OF

Buddhist
Wisdom

Gill Farrer-Halls

A GODSFIELD BOOK

I would like to thank everyone who helped with this book in any way. In particular I am grateful to Ajahn Amaro, Ani Tenzin Palmo, Martine Batchelor, Gaia House, Kathryn Guta, Andrew Haynes, Amy Hollowell, Lynda Marshall, and Richard von Sturmer for their kind assistance. Special thanks to Stephen Batchelor for his wise advice and abundant kindness, and to Robert Beer for his love and wisdom, and for being there.

In Loving Memory of
John Snelling

First published in Great Britain in 2000
by Godsfield Press Ltd
Godsfield House, Old Alresford, Hants SO24 9RQ

10 9 8 7 6 5 4 3 2

© 2000 Godsfield Press
Text © 2000 Gill Farrer-Halls

Designed for Godsfield Press by
The Bridgewater Book Company

Printed and bound in China

ISBN 1–84181–000–2

The publishers wish to thank the following for the use of pictures:
Abhayagiri Buddhist Monastery: pp. 126B, 127; **Martine Batchelor**: pp. 5, 96B, 146T, 147, 148, 149, 164R, 184T, 190;
Robin Bath Photographic: pp. 39, 41, 42–3, 47, 98B, 125B, 128, 129B, 134T, 172, 173, 178, 186T; **Robert Beer**: pp. 51, 98T,
138, 145T, 159T, 186; *The Encyclopedia of Tibetan Symbols and Motifs*, 1999 © Robert Beer: pp. 9, 11, 130–1, 154–5, 178–9;
Bridgeman Art Library: pp. 1, 3, 9T, Christie's Images, London; 11B, 12B, 13, 102B, National Museum of India, New Delhi; 15B, 61,
Oriental Museum, University of Durham; 26B, 28T, Private Collection; 29, British Library, London; 29B, Victoria and Albert
Museum, London; 32–3. Kinkakuji, Kyoto, Japan; **Community of Inter Being**: pp. 152–3, Simon Chaput/*A Joyful Path, Community
Transformation and Peace*, Thich Nhat Hanh and Friends, Parallax Press, Ca., © 1994, Eglise Bouddhique Unifiée;
Ian Cumming: p. 177; **e.t. archive**: pp. 12T, 19B, 27, 184L; **Wolfgang Hurten**: p. 38; **Hutchison Library**: pp. 6–7, 10, 11T, 14–15,
17, 22, 24–5B, 25T, 30, 31, 32T, 33T, 37, 49B, 50, 58T, 59B, 94L, 96T, 102T, 108T, 110, 112T, 113, 116, 117, 120T, 121, 122, 123,
136T, 140T, 142–3, 144, 145B, 158, 159B, 160, 162, 164B, 170B, 175, 183; **Image Bank**: pp. 2, 4, 8, 18, 19, 23, 24T, 26T, 28B, 45,
46, 52, 53, 54, 57, 58–9, 62, 64–80, 84, 86, 88, 90, 100B, 108, 111, 114, 118–19, 120, 129T, 134B, 136B, 140B, 146B, 154B;
Rochester Zen Center: pp. 150–1; **Tibet Images**: pp. 8–9, 20–1, 34, 35, 36, 44, 48, 49T, 55, 56, 82, 92–3,
100T, 112B, 166–7, 168, 169, 170T, 171, 176B, 182, 184R, 186B, 191;
Tony Stone Associates: p. 155T; **Vipassana Trust, UK**: pp. 124–5.
Cover picture: Robert Beer
The publishers wish to thank the following for the use of properties:

The Brighton Buddhist Centre, Brighton; Cargo Homeshop, Brighton;
David Rose Sports Shop, Brighton; Gaia House, Devon.

CONTENTS

66 *You sentient beings who seek deliverance, why do you not let go? When sad, let go of the cause of sadness ... When covetous or lustful, let go of the object of desire. From moment to moment be free of self. Where no self is, there can be no sorrow, no desire ... The winds of circumstance blow across emptiness. Whom can they harm?* 99

CHENG-LI

introduction

When someone becomes interested in Buddhism the obvious question that arises is, "What is Buddhism?" The answer is not so obvious, however, and even experienced Buddhists continue to contemplate this question. One reason there is no simple answer is that a true knowledge of Buddhism comes only from practical experience. This means making some commitment to meditating, reading Buddhist texts, and taking on a teacher: a spiritual friend who can guide us through our questions and doubts. The support of friends who practice Buddhism is also invaluable.

It is good to start simply and not try to run before we can walk. This is clear from a popular saying of the Dalai Lama: "If you can manage to be nice to other people, this is enough." Yet, as we know from our own experience, even this apparently simple practice is difficult if we are tired or angry. So we can see that Buddhism is both a way of life and a state of mind, not merely an intellectual exercise or a label with which we can identify.

Below and right
Chorten near Mount Kailash, the mountain most sacred to Tibetans and Indians. A *chorten* (or dharma support) may hold sacred objects or act as a funerary monument, normally for a prominent person. Buddhists often walk around such structures in a clockwise direction while praying.

Why Practice Buddhism?

The reason people follow Buddhist teachings and practice meditation is to become free from suffering and find happiness. This is summed up in the most well known and fundamental teaching of Buddhism, the Four Noble Truths – which were Buddha's first teaching after he attained enlightenment.

Buddha said that we should test his teachings as we would test gold: subject them to fire and beat them to see if their nature remains pure and true. If we find that they satisfy our personal scrutiny, then it is appropriate to investigate further by exploring meditation and also trying out the wisdom of these Buddhist teachings in our daily lives.

Left
The Buddha was born in fifth-century BCE India. His teachings spread from there across Asia, assimilating the native belief systems of each land so that different traditions exist.

How Buddhism Developed

After Buddha's death, his teachings were interpreted in different ways. They eventually spread throughout Asia and were assimilated into the various cultures of different countries. In this way, separate schools and traditions developed, though all share the same essence. So for a Japanese and a Tibetan, a Sri Lankan and a Vietnamese, Buddhism does not mean exactly the same thing, though all of them would easily recognize each tradition as Buddhist.

"To be thus enlightened is to remove the barriers between one's self and others."

DOGEN

introduction

The various schools of Buddhism traveled further to Europe and America and we now have a rich diversity of Buddhist teachings available here. The following chapters describe the three major traditions of Buddhism, Theravada, Zen, and Tibetan and how they developed. We will also see how these traditions are manifesting in Europe and America by looking at particular Buddhist centers. Over time, as Buddhism in the West becomes conditioned by our culture, new forms will doubtless arise, so we will briefly look at these beginnings, too.

Understanding and Practicing Buddhism

In order to understand what Buddhism is, we need first to know about the life of Shakyamuni Buddha and his basic teachings and philosophy. Next, we need to see how the different traditions arose and what their meditations and practices are. Then we need to know how to do them! As emphasized earlier, Buddhism is a way of life. This book will be as practical as possible so the reader can learn enough to start meditating and reflecting upon the beliefs and ideas behind the practices, as well as learning about what to expect when visiting a Buddhist center.

Buddhism is often mistakenly perceived as being difficult, esoteric, out of date, or exclusively Eastern. However, the essence of Buddhist teachings lies in simple, ordinary guidelines that help us live our lives in harmony with ourselves, others, and our environment. In many Buddhist tales the

"*Our daily lives, the way we eat, drink, walk, all has to do with the world situation.*"

THICH NHAT HANH

Left
Buddhist monks
conduct ceremonies
for the enshrinement
of religious relics
inside chortens like
the Peace Pagoda,
which sits prominently
beside the River
Thames in London's
Battersea Park.

protagonist who becomes enlightened is a
simple, uneducated person. Great teachers are
often renowned for their simplicity and can be
found performing the most humble tasks in
peace and happiness. This book offers practical,
simple ways to transform our lives and is accessible to anyone interested in Buddhism.

Right and Far Left
Revered as having auspicious influ-
ence, symbolic designs decorate
Buddhist religious relics like this
Indian stupa (chorten) and
monastery rooftops (far left).

The Inspiration to Begin

We might not know what attracts us to
Buddhism in the first place; perhaps it is
hearing an inspiring teacher like the Dalai
Lama or encountering a Western Buddhist
teacher. We may have read a book or seen a
film that made us curious, or we may have
traveled to a Buddhist country in Asia. But
however we encounter Buddhism, we all share
the potential to transform our lives and find
peace and happiness through learning about
and practicing Buddhist wisdom. Buddhism is
as fresh and alive today as it was when Buddha
became enlightened and started his timeless
teaching of how to wake up here and now.

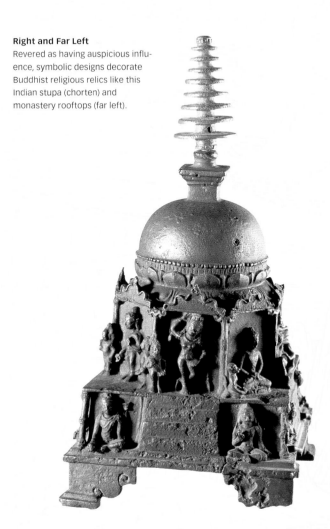

Above
Prince Siddhartha never encountered death until he left the pleasure palace where his father the king protected him. Then he renounced his claim to the throne and followed a spiritual life.

Buddha Shakyamuni was born Siddhartha Gautama into a ruling family of the Shakya clan in Northern India, in about 500 BCE. Shortly after Siddhartha's birth, a wise man called Asita was asked to bless the child and pronounced that he would become either a great religious teacher or a world leader.

Siddhartha's father, Shuddhodana, wanted an heir to rule after him and – much preferring Asita's latter prediction – decided to create a pleasure palace his son would never want to leave. So Siddhartha grew up in luxurious surroundings with his every wish fulfilled. He married the beautiful Yashodhara and had a son, Rahula.

Eventually, this lifestyle bored Siddhartha and he became curious about life outside the palace walls. Shuddhodana permitted his son four trips to the local town but ordered his servants to clear anything unpleasant or ugly out of sight beforehand. However, on the first trip Siddhartha saw an old person, on the second a sick person, and on the third he saw a corpse.

Deeply troubled on each occasion, Siddhartha asked his servant if these things would happen to everyone, including himself. On hearing that everyone was subject to age, sickness, and death Siddhartha realized the pointlessness of his current decadent life and fell into existential despair. However, on his fourth and final visit, he saw a wandering holy man, poverty stricken and wearing rags, but radiant with inner peace.

Right
This statue shows bodhisattva Padmapani Avalokiteshvara, the embodiment of Buddha's compassion. Showing compassion to others is the basic tenet of Buddha's teachings.

Below
A portion of a third or fourth-century Central Asian wall painting showing Buddha expounding the law, accompanied by six disciples.

Embarking on a Spiritual Path

Siddhartha then decided to live a spiritual life and one night fled from the palace. Cutting off his hair and wearing rags, he approached a well-known religious teacher of the day and requested instruction. He learned all he could from this teacher, then moved on and found another. He later practiced extreme asceticism and finally joined a group of five other ascetic yogis.

One day, near death from his extreme fasting, he wandered down to the river to meditate. He had learned many spiritual disciplines but had not found the answers he sought. A girl tending cows offered him a dish of milk and rice and, as the food strengthened his body, he realized that extreme asceticism was no more the answer than his earlier life of sensual indulgence had been and that a middle way was the best course of action. His fellow ascetics left him in disgust because he had eaten.

With renewed strength, Siddhartha sat under a Bodhi tree and resolved not to move until he had attained enlightenment. He entered deep meditation and finally – after wrestling with the demons of desire and ignorance – saw the dawn break with new eyes, free from the duality of life and death. Siddhartha had become enlightened and entered Nirvana, the liberation from cyclic existence.

Realizing everyone else was still trapped in samsara (the cyclic existence of birth, death, and rebirth), Buddha – as he had now become – spent the rest of his life teaching and ordaining those who chose to follow him, creating a set of practical guidelines for living in harmony and working toward freedom from suffering.

He died around the age of eighty from food poisoning, surrounded by his disciples. His last words were: "Impermanent are all created things. Strive on with awareness. . . ."

The Four Noble Truths

uddha's first teaching after enlightenment was the Four Noble Truths. They are the fundamental teaching of Buddhism and so are a good place to start.

The Four Noble Truths

 1 The existence of suffering

2 The causes of suffering

 3 The cessation of the causes of suffering

 4 The path that leads to the cessation of the causes of suffering

Above
Awareness of suffering underlies Buddhist practice, evident in the demeanor of this Thai monk performing a blessing ceremony.

"*Suffering I teach – and the way out of suffering.*"

SHAKYAMUNI BUDDHA

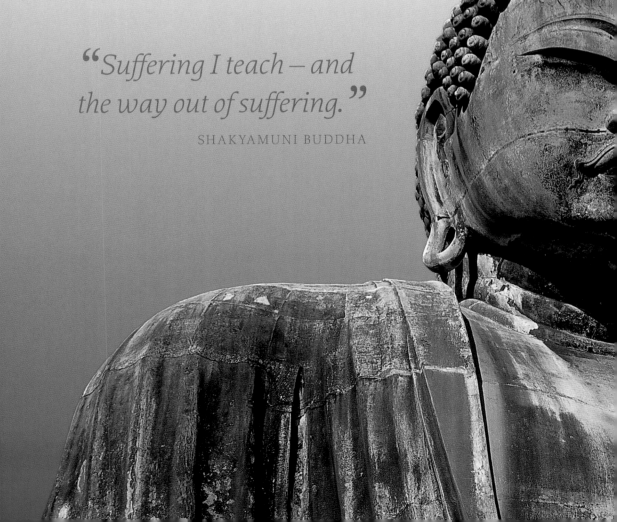

I THE EXISTENCE OF SUFFERING

The Pali word *dukkha* is usually translated as "suffering," but it has a much broader meaning, ranging from "dissatisfaction" to "anguish." We all know that suffering exists and have experienced various degrees of it, but what Buddha means in the first Noble Truth is that suffering permeates our existence, affecting both our minds and bodies.

This may seem a little strange and we might ask, "What about happiness?" But if we look closely at what makes us happy, we notice these things are subject to change. For example, if we are on holiday in the sun and we dive into a pool to get cool, the sensations are at first pleasurable but after a while we are cool enough and we need to get out. If we stay in the pool, we will start to suffer from the cold, tiredness, and so on.

So happiness occurs then disappears – often quite quickly. Dissatisfaction or suffering, however, is present all the time; though when we are happy we may not notice it for a while. This is because – as Siddhartha observed – we are born, get sick, get old, and eventually die. We cannot escape any of these facts: they are integral to life.

If we reflect on this, although we may at first find it unpleasant, we soon see that this is a realistic and not a pessimistic view of existence. This makes us want to investigate the second Noble Truth: the causes of suffering.

Left
Many statues depicting the Buddha are huge in size.

Right
This nineteenth-century Tibetan painting depicts the peaceful and wrathful deities of the Bardo – the visionary realm of the after-death state.

2

THE CAUSES OF SUFFERING

Usually we blame external circumstances for making us suffer but if we look inside ourselves, we discover we are full of desires. We have all said to ourselves, "If only I had this thing, I would be happy." But even if we get our heart's desire, what happens? It only makes us happy for a while. Either we take it for granted, or we get bored with it and no longer want it, or start to desire something else – "If only I had *that* thing . . ." – and so on.

We also notice that we're often as dissatisfied with what we *do* get as with what we don't. We are all familiar with the gross manifestations of success: we want to be rich and famous, adored by the latest film star. In reality we are overdrawn at the bank, well-known only among our friends, and – sometimes – loved by the boy or girl next door. The subtle levels are less obvious: "I want to be good," and "I'd like to help alleviate Third World poverty." These seem like good ideas, but they are still desires and cause us suffering when we can't live up to them. This brings us to the third Noble Truth: the cessation of the causes of suffering.

3

THE CESSATION OF THE CAUSES OF SUFFERING

We now know that the cessation of suffering is possible, which is a relief! The traditional Buddhist term for the cessation of suffering is the Sanskrit word *Nirvana*. Though we may well have heard this word before, we may be confused about what it really means.

It is impossible to explain exactly what Nirvana is if you have not experienced it – imagine trying to describe snow to someone who has never seen it before. More useful is to say what it is not, particularly as misperceptions are common. Most importantly, it is not a Buddhist heaven. Nirvana is not a place, it is an unconditioned state of liberation from suffering. Another common mistake is to think Nirvana is nothing – annihilation – or that it is eternal; but it is beyond either of these extremes.

The fact that Nirvana exists and that Buddha attained this state is an inspiration to try to free ourselves from samsara, this world of desires and suffering, repeated lifetime after lifetime. This leads us to the fourth Noble Truth: the path that leads to the cessation of the causes of suffering.

4

THE PATH THAT LEADS TO THE CESSATION OF THE CAUSES OF SUFFERING

The fourth Noble Truth is a set of guidelines for living in a way that will help liberate us from being driven by our desires and create the causes for us eventually to attain Nirvana. This is the Noble Eightfold Path, which gives us practical ways to lessen desire and suffering.

CONCLUSION

Buddha likened the Four Noble Truths to medicine for a sick person. Firstly, we need to know that we are sick, this is the realization that we are suffering; secondly, we need to identify the diseases making us ill, these are the causes of our suffering; thirdly, we need to believe we can get well, this is realizing the truth of Nirvana; and fourthly, we need a course of medicine to get us on the path to freedom from suffering.

Left
Buddha passed beyond suffering and discovered his true nature or natural state – termed "buddhanature" – which is present in all sentient beings.

What the Four Noble Truths Mean Today

> "*... the ultimate aim of Buddhist practice is to engineer mystical experience: to penetrate the great mystery at the heart of life and find the answers to the knotty problems that have perennially engaged the most developed minds of the human race.*"
>
> JOHN SNELLING

The Buddha's enlightenment and teachings are as relevant to us today as they have always been. We see that even if someone is lucky enough to have every wish fulfilled, this eventually becomes boring and such a person must at some point still confront the issue of what it means to be alive. This is the call to awaken to whom we really are.

Below

Buddhists contemplate reflections on water to understand the nature of mind, considering questions like: Can one ever see oneself? Do we see the moon when we see its reflection? Is the world we perceive a reflection – that is, illusory?

The rest is simply a distraction, however pleasant. Most of us don't have such privileged backgrounds as the Buddha had before his enlightenment, but we can still stand back from the distractions in our life and check out who we really are here and now. We also observe that life is essentially unsatisfactory: we are all born, get sick, age, and die. We cannot change these facts of life. But Buddha shows us that by investigating the causes of our suffering, we can go beyond it. A leading twentieth-century Buddhist teacher Thich Nhat Hanh says: "Life is filled with suffering, but it is also filled with many wonders, like the blue sky, the sunshine, the eyes of a baby." This view shows us the Buddha's "middle way"; not denying that suffering permeates our lives but enjoying simple, natural pleasures.

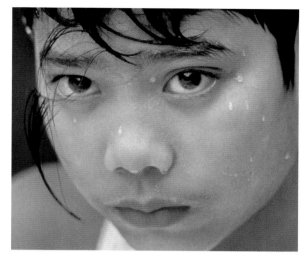

Above

Tulku is the Tibetan term for an enlightened being who has reincarnated out of compassion.

Tulkus were educated in Tibetan monasteries in order to prepare them for spiritual leadership.

BUDDHISM IN ACTION

Buddhism is something to practice, to do, not just the usual religious consolations. We can see this from the last Noble Truth, which is a set of guidelines for action. We must make an effort; salvation lies in our own hands but we have to work toward it. Buddha dedicated his life to helping others and did not simply rest content in Nirvana. So thinking of others and seeing that their needs are just as important as our own is also a part of the Buddhist path.

When the Buddha decided to help other beings because they were suffering, he did not lose the qualities of enlightenment characterized by Nirvana. How he lived his life was an example to others. Buddha was compassionate and wise but behind these qualities was inner peace. The Dalai Lama says: "If you have inner peace, the external problems do not affect your deep sense of peace and tranquility. In that state of mind you can deal with situations with calmness and reason, while keeping your inner happiness." We can find inner peace in our lives by meditating and following the Buddha's guidelines.

Buddha's message is timeless and universal, unconditioned by age, culture, or any other factors. It says that for all those with the precious gift of life there is an opportunity to awaken to our buddhanature.

The classic Buddhist texts tell us that it often takes many lifetimes to reach this state of awareness but they also say that it is possible in this life, because our essential nature is potential buddhahood. And in this way, there is nothing to attain, merely to awaken to this potential in the present moment.

Our buddhanature lies dormant within us and all we need to do is discover our true self by waking up to our buddhanature.

CHAPTER ONE

HOW BUDDHISM DEVELOPED

66 *There is a distinction between the essence of a religion and the superficial, ceremonial, or ritual level. In India, Tibet, China, Japan, or wherever, the religious aspect of Buddhism is the same, but the cultural heritage is different in each country. Thus, in India Buddhism incorporated Indian culture; in Tibet, Tibetan culture; and so on. From this viewpoint, the incorporation of Buddhism into Western culture may also be possible. The essence of the Buddhist teachings does not change; wherever it goes it is suitable; however the superficial aspects – certain rituals and ceremonies – are not necessarily suitable for a new environment; those things will change.* 99

THE DALAI LAMA

Above
The ornate interior of this
Buddhist temple in Colombo
shows the respect accorded to

Buddhism in Sri Lanka, where the
Buddha's teachings were first
written down.

> "Two thousand years
> ago, Indian influences
> spread throughout south
> and southeast Asia, and
> these included all forms of
> Buddhism.... Today we
> find three southern Asian
> countries: Sri Lanka,
> Burma, and Thailand,
> which may still be called
> Buddhist countries in the
> full sense of the term."
>
> JOHN SNELLING

Buddhism inevitably traveled outside of India and around 250 BCE a Theravada Buddhist monk and nun went to Sri Lanka (at that time Ceylon). Mahinda and Sanghamitta were children of the great Emperor Ashoka, so their visit generated much interest, and they were well received by King Devanampiyatissa.

Sri Lanka

Buddhism flourished in Sri Lanka and it was the first place where the Buddha's words were written down. Over the ensuing centuries, other forms of Buddhism also arrived and controversy inevitably developed, but a council held in 1160 upheld the Theravadans and suppressed the other schools. The early Pali scriptures remain the religious texts of Theravada Buddhists today.

Theravada Buddhism still flourishes in Sri Lanka, though European colonization from the sixteenth century onward seriously threatened Buddhism, as efforts were made to convert the indigenous population to Christianity. A Buddhist revival started in the nineteenth century, and a brilliant monk called Gunananda challenged the Christians to a religious debate which the latter lost, heralding their decline.

Above and Right
Theravada Buddhism has been
Sri Lanka's predominant religion
since 1160 CE, when other

Buddhist schools declined. Early
Pali scriptures remain the texts
used today by Theravadans.

Southeast Asia

Above
Buddhism has flourished in Burma
(Myanmar) since its arrival in the
fifth or sixth century, as in this
temple painting in Pagan, Burma.

Burma

Burma was influenced by both Theravada and
Mahayana Buddhism from about the fifth or sixth
century. The Theravadans gained prominence
during the reign of King Anawrahta in the ninth
century and his dynasty, based at Pagan, lasted for
two centuries. Even when his dynasty disintegrated
and Burma split into small warring states,
Buddhism carried on, and many fine temples and
pagodas continued to be built.

The states of Burma were reunited in the eighteenth century, and Buddhism flourished again
under the reign of King Mindon, some fifty years
later. Shortly after this the British arrived and since

Right
Near Kandy, the hill-
country capital of Sri
Lanka, stands this
combined Buddhist and
Hindu site with its fine
Sinhalese architecture.
Although other religions
are present in Sri Lanka,
Theravada Buddhism
predominates.

independence the socialists have been in power. Neither the British nor the socialists encouraged Buddhism but it has nonetheless survived relatively intact. The current opposition leader Aung San Suu Khyi – who is at this point under house arrest – is a devoted Buddhist, so there is the potential for Burma – or Myanmar, as it is now more recently known – to see a Buddhist renaissance.

Left
This sculpture in Indonesia of Buddha surrounded by flowers proves that Buddhism influenced its culture, although it was less dominant there than in Sri Lanka and Burma.

Thailand

It is unclear how Buddhism first appeared in Thailand but it is thought that missionaries from India arrived there in the third century. However, it is possible that the first encounter might have come from the Chinese, who by this time had themselves been exposed to Buddhism from India. However, the Khmers took control a few centuries later and their reign lasted until the fourteenth century.

In the fourteenth century the Thais regained power and brought over monks from Sri Lanka to strengthen the local Buddhism that still existed. Thus Theravada Buddhism predominated and Buddhism remains the state religion. It is also a condition that the king must be Buddhist, but other religions are also tolerated. Because Buddhism is institutionalized there are now two distinguishable forms: the priestly town Buddhists who perform all the usual traditional ceremonies, and the forest monks who devote themselves totally to meditation.

Laos

Buddhism, together with Brahminism, was probably introduced into Laos during the early domination of the Khmers. Thailand later took power, consequently Thai Buddhism prevailed. When the Communists took power in 1975, most of the monks fled. Those who stayed were made to teach Marxism, so authentic Buddhism has virtually disappeared.

Kampuchea

A mixture of Mahayana Buddhism and Brahminism flourished in Kampuchea, formerly Cambodia, from the ninth to fifteenth centuries. Theravada Buddhism developed from the thirteenth century until it was almost totally destroyed by the Communist Khmer Rouge in 1975. Since the Vietnamese invasion in 1979 religion is permitted again.

Indonesia

Since the fifth century, Indonesia favored both Theravada and Mahayana Buddhism, and these took their place alongside Hinduism and other Indian influences. A cult developed in Bali incorporating Buddhism and Shaivism that still exists today. Pure Theravada and Mahayana have recently begun to flourish, and with their revival Indonesia may become a Buddhist country again.

China

Above
Chinese people praying in a Buddhist shrine. Buddhism became popular after similarities with Taoism were discerned and the Han Dynasty fell.

Right
This painting showing a country magistrate's examination conveys the Chinese preference for harmony in social spheres, which was satisfied by Confucianism.

Left
This statue of Avalokiteshvara (the bodhisattva of compassion) comes from Japan's nineteenth-century Edo period.

In the first century, Buddhism started to trickle into China along the Silk Road, but its acceptance and influence were limited. The Chinese believed that their empire was unrivaled in splendor and wisdom and so were naturally unreceptive to most things foreign. The prevailing ideology of the time – Confucianism – suited their need for social harmony, and for those people seeking something more spiritual, there was Taoism. However, as similarities between Taoism and Buddhism were discerned, Buddhism gradually made headway.

When the Han Dynasty collapsed in 220 CE, Buddhism became popular, as the teachings on impermanence seemed particularly relevant. The intellectuals and ruling classes started to prefer Buddhism over Taoism, so it flourished, experiencing a golden age from the sixth to ninth centuries. As monasteries developed even peasants started to be ordained – partly to escape their life of extreme poverty.

"We may be led to critical reflection upon Toynbee's thesis that religion plays a vital role in preserving elements of continuity between a disintegrating civilization and its successor, and that Mahayana Buddhism – as a 'church of the internal proletariat' – played such a role during the break-up of Han civilization."

ARTHUR WRIGHT

China

Three hundred years was long enough for an authentic Chinese Buddhism to emerge. However, even at its peak it was conditioned and influenced by both Taoism and Confucianism, as well as Chinese culture and folk religions, and as a result it was quite different from Indian Buddhism.

Specific schools of Buddhism developed, such as the Vinaya, the Mantra or secret, the Avatamsaka, the White Lotus, Pure Land, and Ch'an (Chinese Zen). This diversity was indicative of both the proliferation of Buddhism and its creative interaction with various forms of Chinese spiritual wisdom.

However, during the latter part of the ninth century, a secular backlash and the resurgence of Confucianism (Neo-Confucianism) heralded a Buddhist decline, gradually causing all but the Pure Land and Ch'an schools to disappear. Ch'an had a brief golden age during the Sung dynasty (960–1279). However, the unconventional spontaneity that inspired Ch'an dwindled into formalized institutionalization, and Ch'an's cultural impact diminished.

Above

China's culture, folk religions, Confucianism, and Taoism | influenced the development of Chinese Buddhism.

Left

Vegetarianism is practiced by some Buddhists throughout the East, but not those influenced by habits of culture or limited food availability like the Tibetans. Here, Buddhists enjoy a vegetarian meal together.

THE DECLINE OF CHINESE BUDDHISM

Buddhism continued to survive in China but it would never see the same level of innovation or numbers of devotees again. In the thirteenth century, Indian Buddhism was wiped out by the Muslim invasions, so no new energy came from that direction. A brief resurgence occurred under the Mongol Yuan dynasty in 1280, which even made Buddhism the state religion, but this form of Buddhism (based on Tibetan Buddhism) proved unpopular with many people and swiftly disappeared.

Marxism proved the most formidable enemy of all. The Marxist belief that Buddhism would naturally decline meant that the Marxist government did not immediately suppress it and merely tried to control it by forming the Chinese Buddhist Association. However, they discouraged the practice of Buddhism even within this organization, and it was only a matter of time before Buddhism gradually faded away.

The Communist and Cultural Revolutions of the twentieth century brutally ravaged what remained of Buddhism. Most Buddhist temples and monasteries were sacked and monastics forced to disrobe. Since 1976, when China allowed access to the West again, there has been a gradual, but steadily growing, tolerance toward Buddhism again. Temples have been rebuilt and those wishing to practice and even ordain can now do so. A more liberal regime has even "regretted" the earlier excesses, and today religion is permitted,

though not encouraged. However, Buddhism is still regarded by some to be "poison" – Chairman Mao's famous decree.

China's continued interaction with the West includes adoption of certain capitalist ideas. Materialism and consumerism intermingle with Communism, and this may ultimately prove a subtle but effective enemy of Buddhism.

Right
This image shows Hvasang (Huang Tsang), a Chinese Buddhist pilgrim to India.

Above
In Buddhism everyday life is as important as meditation and religious ritual. Here, vegetables are being sorted for the day's meals in the Zen community at Bukkokoji Monastery, Japan.

The golden age of Buddhism started in the first century with the conversion of the Kushan Kings. This coincided with the founding of their great empire, which incorporated parts of northern India, Chinese Turkestan, Afghanistan, and Russia. However, after the fifth century, Buddhism in this area declined. In contrast to southeast Asia, where orthodox Theravada Buddhism took root, it was Mahayana Buddhism, arising some time after Buddha's death, that prevailed in the Far East.

Buddhism traveled the Silk Road alongside traders and travelers, encountering different cultures. The northwest of the Indian subcontinent,

"Kanishka's reign … marked a turning point in the history of Buddhism and Buddhist literature. It witnessed the rise of Mahayana Buddhism … It was during Kanishka's reign and largely through his efforts that Buddhism was successfully introduced into central and eastern Asia."

BHARAT SINGH UPADHYAYA

Left
This sculpture conveys the mood of contemplative, quietly joyful, internalized peace, which Zen Buddhist practitioners may experience.

Right
The ordered asceticism of Zen Buddhism is shown in this central hall of a Zen monastery in Butsuden, Japan.

The Far East

Above

Small Buddhas beneath this Buddha with two bodhisattvas illustrate the belief that everyone has buddhanature – that is, the ability to combine wisdom and compassion in enlightened activity.

including parts of Kashmir, Pakistan, Afghanistan, and Central Asia, witnessed another great flowering of Mahayana Buddhism. This area was called Serindia – literally "Silk India." However, the glaciers that irrigated the region dried up and by the seventh century this area was deserted.

Chinese political dominance ensured that Buddhism also spread to Korea and Vietnam, where mostly Zen traditions arose – though Vietnam was also influenced by Theravada Buddhism from southeast Asia. Internal and external upheavals have been disruptive but South Korean and Vietnamese Buddhism are both well established.

Japan

Japan saw Buddhism arrive in the sixth century, mainly from China. The established folk religion, Shinto, was initially resistant, but Buddhism was favorably received by the rulers of the time. Various schools of Buddhism gradually arose, including the tantric Shingon and the philosophical Tendai, as well as Zen and devotional schools.

The Kamakura period (1185–1333) saw the samurai warriors seize power from the ruling classes and set up a military governorship, or

Shogunate. Shingon and Tendai Buddhism did not fit in, but Zen and Pure Land Buddhism (a devotional school) prospered. The two major Japanese Zen schools arose at this time: Eisai transmitting Rinzai and Dogen transmitting Soto. So, despite being politically unstable, this was a fruitful age for Buddhism. The devotional Pure Land brought Buddhism to the masses, and women were also seen to have spiritual potential.

By the end of the Kamakura period in 1333 Buddhism was well established but its creative age was over. Economic prosperity and later civil strife occupied more attention. Then, in the mid-sixteenth century, the warlord Nubunaga destroyed the three thousand temples at Mount Hiei, killing all the monks. Neo-Confucianism became the official policy and Japan was shut off to the outside world. Buddhism survived but languished under state control.

Above
Japan's Pure Land Buddhism, which emerged during the Kamakura period (1185–1333), encouraged a shift in Japanese perspective in which women were also seen to have spiritual potential.

Left
This fifteenth-century temple, dedicated to the shogun Ashikaga Yoshimitus (1358–1408), indicates how Japan mixed religion with economic concerns and civil war.

In 1868 Japan once again restored an imperial regime. It also opened up to the rest of the world and became more modernized. The Buddhists were at first persecuted but once it was realized how entrenched Buddhism had become, religious freedom was granted.

Some Japanese Buddhist schools, including Nichiren, tended toward national militancy and helped lead Japan into the Second World War. However, after Japan's defeat, the lay oriented Nichiren tradition Soka Gakkai – notable for not supporting Japan's involvement in the war – gained increasing popularity and mass appeal, partly for promoting peace through Buddhism. Rinzai, Soto, and Pure Land are also still practiced.

Tibet

The great Indian Buddhist teacher Shantarakshita and the tantric adept Padmasambhava introduced the teachings into Tibet in the eighth century, invited by King Trisong Detsen. An earlier king, Songsten Gampo, had laid the foundations by marrying two Buddhist wives, one Chinese and one Nepalese, which was also a skillful political move. Their Buddhist devotion inspired an interest in the religion.

Shantarakshita was asked to build the first Buddhist monastery at Samye but had problems with the local spirits and demons. Tibet had its own indigenous animistic religion called Bon, full of magic, mystery, and spirits, and these were naturally resistant to this new foreign religion.

Above
The Potala, the palace of the Dalai Lama, Tibet's spiritual and temporal head, dominates Lhasa in central Tibet even today, while its once-sacred streets are now full of brothels and gambling halls.

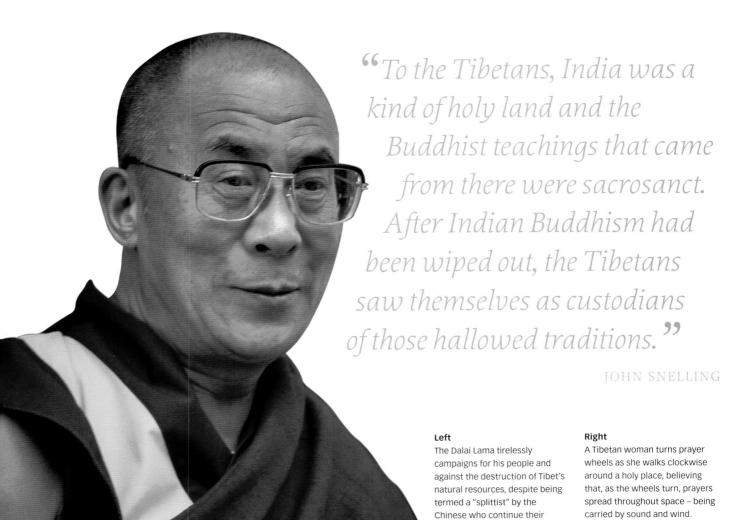

" *To the Tibetans, India was a kind of holy land and the Buddhist teachings that came from there were sacrosanct. After Indian Buddhism had been wiped out, the Tibetans saw themselves as custodians of those hallowed traditions.* "

JOHN SNELLING

Left
The Dalai Lama tirelessly campaigns for his people and against the destruction of Tibet's natural resources, despite being termed a "splittist" by the Chinese who continue their oppression of the Tibetans.

Right
A Tibetan woman turns prayer wheels as she walks clockwise around a holy place, believing that, as the wheels turn, prayers spread throughout space – being carried by sound and wind.

Tibet

Above
Tibetan refugees escaping Chinese persecution settled at Dharamsala, where the Dalai Lama has resided │ since India's Prime Minister Nehru (1947–64) gave him political asylum.

Padmasambhava was a great tantric yogi and able to subdue the local spirits. Tantra is the mystical transformative aspect of Buddhism, and Padmasambhava challenged the highest Bon priests to a spiritual duel of religious debate and psychic

power. Padmasambhava won and Buddhism spread throughout Tibet – though influenced by Bon.

In the ninth century, due to a successful anti-Buddhist movement by King Langdarma, Buddhism was suppressed. The second transmission in the eleventh century again saw great teachers come from India: Atisha and Naropa, also the Tibetan Marpa, who taught Tibet's most famous yogi or "saint," Milarepa. Buddhism entered a renaissance where learning and sacred art thrived until the thirteenth century, when the notorious Genghis Khan began to vanquish the countries of central Asia.

Tibet proved no exception and fell to the Mongols. However, they made a deal with one of the Tibetan Buddhist sects and Buddhism remained unpersecuted. Power returned to the Tibetans as Mongol influence waned in the fourteenth century, but another alliance with a different sect in the sixteenth century caused infighting between the different sects. In the eighteenth century the Chinese replaced the Mongol protectorate, but this remained a formality, and Tibet stayed independent and Buddhist.

Left
Here, people spin prayer wheels in a Lhasa temple. The Chinese destroyed over three thousand Buddhist monasteries in Tibet, and have rebuilt others, which are showcases for tourists rather than religious institutions.

THE CHINESE INVASION

The Chinese Communist invasion started in 1950, though it was formally announced on the radio only when the Chinese arrived in the capital, Lhasa, in September 1951. An uneasy situation deteriorated further and in March 1959 the Dalai Lama was forced to flee Tibet.

The slow dismantling of Tibetan government and the suppression of Buddhism was exacerbated during the Cultural Revolution and degenerated into a bloodbath. Most of the monasteries were smashed up and the monastics were forced to disrobe; frequently they were imprisoned and often killed.

Currently, Tibetan Buddhism is permitted by the Chinese authorities but it is difficult to practice seriously, and monasteries are often only tourist showcases. Many of the traditional Tibetan buildings in Lhasa have been bulldozed and replaced by Chinese architecture. Though this has brought improved drainage, Lhasa has tragically lost its Tibetan identity.

Tibetan Buddhism traveled to Mongolia, parts of Russia, and Buryat, also the Himalayan kingdoms of Sikkim, Ladakh, and Bhutan. Neighboring Nepal absorbed Indian Buddhism and had some influence over the development of Tibetan Buddhism. Though these countries culturally adapted Buddhism, developing their own distinct styles, there were no major innovations.

After the demise of the Soviet Union there has been a Buddhist revival in Mongolia, parts of Russia, and Buryat, which had been religiously persecuted under the Soviet Communist regime.

Below

As well as suppressing Buddhism, the Chinese are also destroying Tibetan architecture and rebuilding in Chinese style, even in places most sacred to the Tibetans.

The West

Above
Many young people in Western countries became fascinated by Buddhism in the 1960s. Some went on to develop a genuine understanding of it.

Right
Various incidents in the Buddha's lifetimes are portrayed in stone on London's Peace Pagoda, inside which sacred objects and prayers are housed.

Although Western cultures were aware of Buddhism for centuries, serious interest did not arise until around 155 years ago. Western Christians were concerned more with trying to convert such heathen idolaters than listening to what they had to say. Eventually, however, the more discerning scholars and archeologists sent to examine Eastern cultures became curious.

The Theosophical Society, formed in 1875 by Madame Blavatsky, drew extensively upon Buddhism and brought it to a wider audience. Theosophy was a response to a disillusionment with Western rational materialism and the stagnation of Christianity, reasons that still attract people to Buddhism today.

In the 1960s, Western youth culture flowered into the hippie movement – characterized by a search for peace and a meaning to life beyond what conventional society had to offer. Many people traveled east and encountered Buddhism, and Buddhism also traveled west. Theravada bhikkhus came from Sri Lanka, D.T. Suzuki brought Zen, and the forced exile of Tibetan lamas meant Tibetan Buddhism became available, too.

"[In] the West we are seeing the awakening of the Buddha, and the Buddha is smiling very broadly, with the wisdom of Tibet, India, Japan, Thailand, Burma, and America all joined in. We have been given the treasury of Buddhist practices, a cornucopia of compassion and wisdom to nourish and awaken us to our True Nature."

JACK KORNFIELD

The West

Currently there are over one thousand Buddhist meditation centers in America and a similar number throughout Europe. Many of these follow a pure Theravada, Zen, or Tibetan tradition. However, all traditions are now available simultaneously – thanks to modern communication – so people can also benefit from a more eclectic approach, drawing their inspiration from different schools.

How Western Buddhism Has Developed

Perhaps the major difference between Asian and Western Buddhism lies in the roles of monastic and lay practitioners. Eastern Buddhist societies maintain the tradition of large monasteries supported by a lay community. There are Western monastics and monasteries, which are invaluable and keep the Asian traditions purely, but these days most Western Buddhists are not monastic.

Above
Gaia House, a Western, non-ecumenical Buddhist center in Newton Abbot, Devon, England, offers "insight meditation," encouraging people to "develop self-enquiry and understanding through mindful practice."

Below
Western Buddhists often attend meditation retreats in Gaia House, where different Buddhist meditation techniques are practiced.

Right
One of the chief concerns of Buddhists is the expression of compassion toward others. This may manifest in innumerable ways, as here where two people look after a terminally ill woman. A number of Buddhists are social workers but they may just as easily "help" in less obvious ways.

Many Buddhists are women. Because of the different role of women in the West there has been a softening of the patriarchal Asian Buddhist models, and as a result there are many women teachers. The modern Western ego is psychologically mature and this is reflected in the creative interaction between Buddhism and psychotherapy.

New trends in Western Buddhism include social action, so we see Buddhist chaplains in prisons, Buddhists working with the terminally ill and the homeless, and Buddhist ecology and political activism. Thich Nhat Hanh developed Engaged Buddhism, which he describes thus: "Engaged Buddhism does not only mean to use Buddhism to solve social and political problems. First of all we have to bring Buddhism into our daily lives."

There are the beginnings of formalized Western Buddhism in organizations like the Friends of the Western Buddhist Order, which draws from Western philosophy and art as well as from Buddhism. The Order was founded by the Englishman Sangharakshita who studied Buddhism in India.

Yet these are early days, and we can see from the history of Buddhism in other cultures that this is a formative stage for Western Buddhism. It is a highly creative period and there are Western Buddhist writers, artists, and teachers alongside their Asian counterparts. It is an extraordinarily fertile time for Buddhism and we have the privilege of witnessing – and participating in, if we choose – another great flowering of the wisdom Buddha taught many years ago.

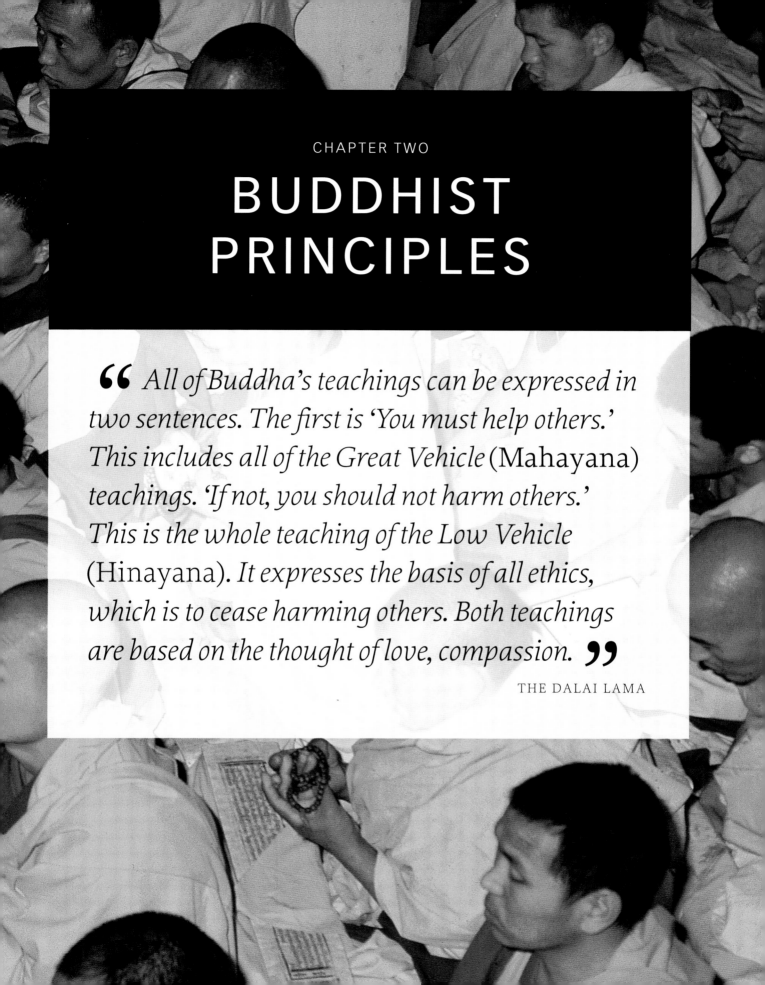

CHAPTER TWO

BUDDHIST PRINCIPLES

> **66** *All of Buddha's teachings can be expressed in two sentences. The first is 'You must help others.' This includes all of the Great Vehicle* (Mahayana) *teachings. 'If not, you should not harm others.' This is the whole teaching of the Low Vehicle* (Hinayana). *It expresses the basis of all ethics, which is to cease harming others. Both teachings are based on the thought of love, compassion.* **99**

THE DALAI LAMA

What it Means to be a Buddhist

Above
Meditating in a cave is a traditional way to seek enlightenment in Tibetan Buddhist practices.

Modern teachers say, however, that your "cave" may be anywhere – in an office or even outdoors.

Buddhism is not a belief system or an abstract philosophy. It is a way of life, with teachings on how to behave and qualities to cultivate. Its methodology is meditation, something we practice rather than study. By following the Buddhist path we aim to awaken to our true nature, the enlightened qualities of a Buddha.

Prince Siddhartha renounced all his possessions and pleasures, and we too need to develop a sense of renunciation. Luckily, this does not necessarily mean abandoning everything and living in a cave for years! Though, if this is what

"*The way of the Buddha is to know yourself.*"

DOGEN

Above
Buddhists observe that, just as water flows over our hands, changes occur in life, no matter what we do. The key to happiness is being able to appreciate this simple truth.

we choose, we are following a pure and authentic Buddhist path.

Renunciation means lessening both our attachment to those things we like and our aversion to unpleasant situations and feelings, by realizing that none of these things have an inherent ability to make us happy or unhappy.

Accepting Desire and Aversion

As Buddhists we can still have nice things and enjoy them, but when they are taken away, we accept it and do not get upset. We try not to be greedy or to seek too hard to satisfy our desires. We can learn to live with and accept our desires without the obsession to satisfy them immediately. At the same time, we can learn to accept disagreeable things without fighting against them. We can rest in the knowledge that whatever bothers us is impermanent and will pass.

A tightly closed fist tries to grasp hold of things, but they slip away because of this grasping. If we open our hands, things pour over and move on unimpeded. In this way, by not trying to control the natural flow of life, we can enjoy it. When we loosen our grasping we become open, which makes us receptive to our environment. We can appreciate other people and our surroundings beyond our tightly held perceptions.

Everyone seeks happiness but as Shakyamuni Buddha said, "There is no way to happiness – happiness is the way." Living a life guided by compassion and wisdom will help us to find happiness in the here and now.

Common Misperceptions

Above
Many Buddhists consider diet to be culturally conditioned, although vegetarianism is considered to be an appropriate expression of the Buddha's teaching on not harming others.

When we first encounter Buddha's teachings the ideas can seem so wonderful that we think being a Buddhist will make us special or different in some way. But as the quotation below suggests, we should not lose sight of the ordinary; we are normal and share the same nature as all other beings. The only difference is that we have the opportunity to awaken to our buddhanature through listening to the teachings and applying them in our lives. Therefore we do not have to dress differently, or shave our heads, or appear different from others – unless we choose to become a nun or a monk.

"*How easy it is to lose ourselves in fascination with the uncanny and forget the ordinariness of it all!*"

STEPHEN BATCHELOR

Being vegetarian is an appropriate expression of the Buddha's teaching on not harming others, but it is not essential. Diet is culturally conditioned. Tibetans eat meat because it is difficult to grow vegetables in their climate. Theravada Buddhists depend on alms and therefore eat whatever they are given. Chinese Buddhists, and Buddhists in the traditions that developed from Ch'an, such as Korean, are usually strictly vegetarian.

We must each choose for ourselves whether to be vegetarian or not. Food in the West is plentiful. This has caused obsession over food, reflected in diseases like bulimia and anorexia. Buddhism emphasises a middle way approach, eating moderately, and this is perhaps most important.

The Buddhist View of Death

Buddhism is sometimes thought to be gloomy and pessimistic because it teaches us to look at the inevitability of death. However, realizing we will die encourages us to make the most of our lives. Then we investigate what Buddha said would make us happy and try to live according to his teachings.

Buddhism is not a theistic religion, and Buddha was not a creator God, as in Christianity. Nirvana is not heaven; it is a state of enlightenment that can be experienced here and now. An enlightened being – a Buddha, or Bodhisattva – can rest in Nirvana or purposefully enter the world to benefit all other beings. Thus Nirvana is not a place, it is the extinguishing of suffering, delusion, and craving.

Taking Refuge in the Three Jewels

"*Taking refuge in the Three Jewels means fully opening our mind to the Jewel of Buddha, by understanding that Buddhas, or Enlightened Ones, are our perfect guides; to the Jewel of Dharma, the teachings shown by Buddha, by understanding that it is the perfect path leading us as well as others beyond suffering; to the Jewel of Sangha, or spiritual friends, by understanding that they are fully qualified in helping us improve our inner understanding through their great inspiration.*"

GHESHE WANGCHEN

When we commit ourselves to the Buddhist path, we first take refuge in the Three Jewels. This means relying upon them for guidance. Normally we take refuge in external objects – for example, when we are hungry we take refuge in food – but these bring only temporary satisfaction. The Buddha, Dharma, and Sangha are inner resources, and are reliable objects of refuge.

We take refuge in the Buddha because he has gone beyond suffering and developed great wisdom and compassion. Buddha has no partiality and wishes to help everyone, no matter who they are

Left
The first formal commitment to Buddhism is taking the refuge vow – to strengthen one's own buddhanature and to reinforce one's resolve to study and practice the Buddha's teachings.

or what they have done. There are as many ways to teach people as there are human dispositions, so the Buddha can guide each individual according to need.

Refuge in the Buddha alludes to being open to and relying upon the limitless love, compassion, and wisdom of those who have attained enlightenment. It also means cultivating our own potential buddhanature, seeds of enlightenment within us.

In order to be free of suffering, we must first know what it is and understand what the causes are. This means training our minds by following the teachings. We take refuge in the Dharma, the true protection from suffering, by developing wisdom from our study and practice of the Buddha's teachings.

Refuge in the Dharma is trusting that the teachings of the Buddha will ultimately lead us to enlightenment, by following the methods he taught. It also means developing our own inner wisdom that tells us what is right and wrong.

Without inspiration from our more advanced spiritual friends and teachers, we are likely to experience many disheartening problems that make it

Above
Tibetan Buddhist monasteries teach young monks the Tibetan language so that they may have greater access to the wealth of knowledge available to them in ancient Buddhist texts.

Above
Taking refuge in the Sangha means that one shares questions and finds answers with people who approach Buddhist philosophy and practices as seriously as one does oneself.

difficult to maintain our Dharma practice and meditation. So we take refuge in the Sangha and follow their example when we have problems.

Refuge in the Sangha refers to our spiritual friends. By talking together we can share experiences, find answers to questions, and resolve problems. Meditating together is inspiring and develops faith. Refuge in the Sangha is also recognizing that we too can help our friends.

Cultivating our Attitude

To take refuge fully in the Three Jewels we need to cultivate two qualities of mind. We must first really wish to be free from suffering. We can think of this in terms of our current life or of not being reborn in the lower realms in future lives. We must also sincerely believe that the Three Jewels can help us. Then we have really taken refuge.

The Wheel of Life

The Wheel of Life depicts how we are trapped in samsara. At the center of the Wheel are three animals, symbolic of the three poisons. They are shown head to tail eating each other, which symbolizes endless cycles of suffering, with one poison causing the next.

The pig represents ignorance, blindness, and delusion. This refers to our erroneous perception of how the world exists; we believe things exist independently and provide lasting satisfaction. We also believe that we exist concretely, rather than in dependence on our different components and external conditions.

This ignorance of how things exist leads to desire, represented by the cock. We mistakenly believe a desired object will bring us enduring happiness. So desire, craving, and lust arise, which cause us suffering, because no sooner do we get what we want than we want something else.

Unsatisfied desire leads to hatred and anger, symbolized by the snake. Because we believe ourselves to exist independently, we place fulfilling our own desires above the well-being of others. So when we don't get what we want, we feel hatred or anger toward someone who has the object we crave.

Anger and hatred prevent us from thinking clearly. So when we suffer these feelings we are unable to change our erroneous perception of how things exist, which keeps us in ignorance . . .

Is there an end to this self-perpetuating suffering? If we look at the picture we see Buddha at the top left, standing outside the Wheel of Life pointing to the moon. He symbolizes liberation from ignorance, desire, and hatred – the causes of suffering. Taking refuge in the Three Jewels helps free us from the three poisons and the five hindrances.

The Five Hindrances

Buddha described five mental states which hinder our spiritual progress and perpetuate suffering. They are: (1) sensual desire, (2) ill will, (3) sloth and torpor, (4) worry and restlessness, and (5) confused doubt.

As well as following the Buddha's path generally, we can also apply specific remedies. For instance, if we feel overwhelming desire for another person, we can lessen our suffering by meditating on the repulsive nature of his or her body. We can visualize what the body is composed of and that it will decompose at death. We can consciously direct goodwill at someone toward whom we feel ill will. We can meditate that this person also wishes to be happy and avoid suffering, just as we do.

Sloth and torpor are best overcome by eating less and taking more exercise. Worry and restlessness often arise from an uneasy conscience, so repenting any negative actions and resolving to not do them again lessens worry. This is the purpose of Catholic confession and psychotherapy, both summed up with the saying "a problem shared is a problem halved."

Confused doubt, as opposed to skeptical questioning, which is useful, is best cured by further practice and study of Buddha's teachings. As we saw with worry, talking things over with like-minded spiritual friends can help clarify particular issues and help you make positive decisions.

> "*When we are unhappy and dissatisfied, we easily become frustrated and this leads to feelings of hatred and anger.*"
>
> THE DALAI LAMA

Below
This image shows a twentieth-century Sino-Tibetan painting of the Wheel of Life.

Karma

"*Linguistically karma means action; specifically it refers to willed actions of body, speech, and mind. All such actions, barring alone those of a buddha … produce subtle seeds which in time will spawn further consequences.*"

JOHN SNELLING

Karma is often called the law of cause and effect. This means that every action we undertake creates a cause that will at some point in time – even in a future rebirth – have an effect. If we do something bad, we will experience negative results; if we do something good, we will experience positive results.

In this way karma operates ethically. This can be useful in helping us behave mindfully, because we know if we do something bad, our karma will sooner or later ripen and we will experience the fruits of our negative action.

As we develop compassion through Buddhist practice, our behavior becomes naturally more ethical, and we become motivated to benefit others, not simply to accumulate karmic points for ourselves. Karma is not a bank account of credits and debits! Buddha implied that it works on subtle levels and there is no knowing when a particular

Two Categories of Action

Karma is more than a moral yardstick, however, and as with all Buddhist practices the motivation is to realize enlightenment and so escape the cycle of birth and death. To this end, all actions are grouped into two classes according to the nature of their motivations and results. They are not seen or judged as intrinsically good or bad.

Samsaric acts are those that arise from ignorance and the conflicting emotions that ignorance produces. They all result in future rebirth. Whether this is a good rebirth, like a precious human rebirth, or a bad one into a hell realm depends on whether the actions are wholesome and meritorious, or unwholesome and non-meritorious.

Acts that lead to liberation are those that are wholesome and also motivated by the desire to be free from samsara. Though they will produce happiness, this is not the point and is not specially valued, because all samsaric happiness is fleeting and impermanent by nature. The point is to be free from samsara altogether. Liberation from birth and death is what gives lasting happiness, and therefore actions that are both wholesome and motivated by the wish to awaken are the best to cultivate. These will eventually lead us to Nirvana.

action will ripen. Indeed, to counter any tendency to store up karmic credits to gain short-term benefit, the Buddhist texts indicate that most actions in our present life will not bear fruit until a future life.

We accrue karma through actions of body, speech, and mind, and the motivations underlying them and the results arising from them. From this we can see how important the intention behind a deed can be. Lesser and greater effects are experienced depending on how complete an action is.

An action is complete when intention, action, and result happen. If any of these are not present, the karmic effect is less. So if we tread on an insect by mistake, without intention, and we are sad at the result, the karmic effect is less than if we stamped on it and were pleased at its death.

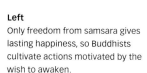

Rebirth

"*Rebirth... should not be confused with reincarnation, which is the view that there is a soul or subtle essence imprinted with an enduring personal stamp that transmigrates or commutes from body to body down through the eons. Buddhism of course rejects that view. What it does admit, however, is causal connection between one life and another.*"

JOHN SNELLING

Above
The image of a butterfly emerging
from a cocoon is a powerful
symbol of death and rebirth.

Rebirth is a causal link between one life and the next, not a soul reincarnating. Only a causal connection links one life to another, so our karmic accumulation conditions our next life. The Buddhist texts illustrate this with an analogy. The flame of a dying candle lights a new candle and then peters out. The new candle is alight but is it the same flame? It is actually neither the same nor a different flame, there has simply been a transference of energy from one object to another.

Contemplating rebirth helps us accept our own death without falling into the two extremes of eternalism or nihilism. Reflecting upon the inevitable fact of our own death encourages us to live our lives well and make the most of our time in this life.

We can consider that we are continuously dying and being reborn from moment to moment. Science shows us that the individual cells which make up our bodies replace themselves every few hours or days. Also, when we wake up each morning, it is like being reborn.

This aspect of rebirth is more constructive than speculating about previous or future lives, because it keeps our attention in the here and now. Buddhism talks about the preciousness of human rebirth because we have the opportunity to wake up to our buddhanature in this moment.

The Realms of Existence

The Buddhist teachings on rebirth describe different realms of existence, including hell realms and the animal and hungry ghost realms, most of which are full of unbearable suffering. There are also delightful god realms of both form gods and formless gods, and there is the human realm too.

All these realms are impermanent, though some last many eons, and we are reborn into one or other of these according to the karma that ripens at the time of our death. The descriptions of the hell realms are designed to make us fear being reborn there, so are useful to help us live ethically.

Descriptions of the god realms remind us that they are wonderful but that even if we are born there, we will eventually die and could be reborn in a lower realm. This teaching helps us realize that samsara is impermanent and that liberation from all cyclic existence is more beneficial than seeking an impermanent lesser happiness.

Our precious human rebirth is the only realm where we have the opportunity to awaken and is therefore the best. Even though we experience suffering, this is an incentive to break free from samsara. Buddha gave the analogy of a blind turtle only surfacing once every hundred years in a vast ocean, on the surface of which floated a small golden yoke. He compared the likelihood of the turtle putting its head through the yoke with that of obtaining a precious human rebirth. So we should seek liberation now, in this lifetime, as another opportunity may not arise for a very long time.

Below
Monk lighting butter lamps in the Jokhang Temple, Lhasa. The flame of an old candle that lights a new candle is neither the same nor a different flame. Energy has simply been transferred.

Impermanence

" *Anything thai is born doesn't stay permanently in one state, it grows up, gets old, and then dies. All things in nature, even the universe itself, have their spans of existence, birth and death, beginning and ending. All that we perceive and can conceive of is change; it is impermanent. So it can never permanently satisfy you.* "

AJAHN SUMEDHO

Below

If something exists long enough, it changes and grows old. Buddhism teaches that old age, sickness, and death are unavoidable and are the natural consequences of birth, health, and life.

Impermanence is one of the classic Buddhist Three Marks of Existence, along with suffering and the doctrine of non-self. Impermanence, called *anicca*, is easily verifiable from our own experience. Some things change so quickly we can almost watch them disintegrate, like an apple in the fruit bowl that rots in a few days. Other phenomena take much longer, as when we watch a stream wash over a stone and get a sense that it will eventually be worn down.

Phenomena are inherently impermanent because they come into being dependent on conditions, and these same conditions cause their dissolution. They are temporal, existing in a moment of time, and however short or long, the conditions that brought about their existence will change, and therefore the object will change, or cease to be.

There is something deeply poignant about impermanence, and the brevity of existence encourages us to value it more. Impermanence has been celebrated by poets and playwrights over the centuries from the Romantic Keats: "She dwells with Beauty – Beauty that must die" to the Existentialist Beckett: "Born astride a grave." This latter haunting image neatly sums up the Buddhist view of things and events carrying with them the seeds of their own demise from birth.

Below
Buddhists observe in nature how even something as solid as stone may be eroded by wind and rain.

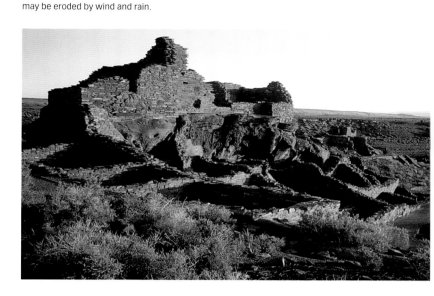

AN ANTIDOTE TO ATTACHMENT

Meditation on impermanence is a great help in lessening our attachment. If we examine why we feel attachment to people and objects it is because we invest them with a sense of unchanging reality. If we are infatuated with someone, we feel strong desire for them as they exist at that time. Yet the person is changing moment to moment and might look and behave differently in a few weeks, let alone a few years. Regular meditation on impermanence lessens our attachment and therefore lessens the suffering we experience in relation to other people and phenomena. It is also useful to meditate on our own impermanence, that we too are changing moment to moment, affected by our own cellular life and by whatever conditions we encounter. When we are not aware of the impermanent nature of our life, we are easily fooled by the desire for pleasure and attachment to happiness. Happiness is short-lived and interspersed with unhappiness. So though we should enjoy happiness when it arises, if we remember it will shortly change, we will not become attached to the pleasant feelings it engenders. Thus when it is inevitably replaced by dissatisfaction, we experience less suffering.

Awareness of impermanence keeps us on the Buddha's path. We are less distracted by people, objects, and events because we know it is in their nature to arise and pass. We naturally spend time reflecting on Buddha's teachings and seeing their relevance in our life.

Buddha once said that just as the elephant's footprint is the biggest of all animal footprints, so meditation on impermanence is the most powerful meditation.

Death

Above
Burning a body in Kathmandu, Nepal. Death is as certain as our birth and is only a breath away.

Buddhists, realizing how fragile and precious life is, seek to live life with awareness.

" Anyone who has a body knows for sure they were born and are going to die and can see it with their own eyes... "

JONGMOK SUNIM

Death is a subject we generally don't think about much unless it comes to someone we know. However, it is certain we will die, and the time and manner of our death are uncertain. Yet we tend to live our lives as if we are sure we will live to be old and die peacefully in our sleep. We don't consider how fragile our life-force is, dependent on all our body systems working together harmoniously. Life – or death – is only a breath away.

Meditating on the certainty of our death paradoxically allows us to live our lives fully, enjoying what each moment has to offer. The sudden play of light and shadow as the sun goes behind a cloud, a burst of birdsong, and a smile all seem more significant when we realize they might be the last we will experience before we die.

Buddha's Story
The Buddha told a story about a grief-stricken woman who came to see him, clutching the corpse of her baby boy. She told him she had waited many years to have a child, and now that he had died at such a young age she was inconsolable. She asked the Buddha to work a miracle and bring her son back to life.

Buddha smiled compassionately at her, aware of her terrible grief, and thought awhile of the best way to help her. Then he told her if she would bring him a mustard seed from each household in the village where no one had died, he would see what he could do. The woman brightened considerably at this news, thanked him, and still carrying the corpse of her baby went off to the village.

All day long she knocked on doors and asked, "Has no one died here?" and told her tale by way of explanation. However, she found not a single household where a family member had not died. As evening fell she was exhausted and had not one mustard seed for all her efforts. She sat down and pondered upon the Buddha's request and what lesson it might teach her.

She thought, "Is this not the nature of all living things? All who are born must as surely die." Gradually she realized the teaching Buddha had given her was this basic fact of life but one that was hard to learn. The understanding she reached through the skill and wisdom of the Buddha allowed her to accept the death of her child.

Whether rich or poor, good or bad, young or old, we are all equally powerless when death arrives. We cannot take any material possessions nor loved ones with us. All our wonderful experiences are gone forever. The only thing of any use when we die is a calm mind, so we can face death with peace. Now is the time to listen to Buddha's teaching and practice meditation to train our mind, and to awaken before this precious human life is gone.

Left and Below
People in Eastern countries are reminded of death by outdoor cremations (left) and places like the Manikarnika funeral ghat on the Ganges River in Varanasi, India (below). In the West, we deceive ourselves by keeping death behind closed doors.

Interdependence

"If Buddhism makes no appeal to the idea of a creator God and if things are not self-creating, how do phenomena arise?"

JOHN SNELLING

We have seen that karma is the doctrine of cause and effect. Interdependence, or dependent origination, explains this further by showing that all phenomena – including ourselves – are produced by causes contained within our universe. From the Buddhist view, there is no external agent; all things are caused by previous things and go on to be causes of other or future things. Dependent origination, called *pratitya samutpada*, therefore means that each phenomenon depends on the various causes and conditions that brought it into existence. Without them, it simply could not exist. A flower, for example, depends on a seed, the person who planted it, and the soil, sun, and rain that allowed it to germinate and grow. These are the causes and conditions without which the flower would not exist – it has no existence apart from them.

There is a beautiful image that describes interdependence, called Indra's Jewelled Net. Think of a clear and cloudless dark night sky with millions of twinkling stars. Then imagine fine lines connecting each star with every other star. This is like Indra's Net, where each jewel is reflected in every other jewel; the whole is dependent on all the parts. If even one jewel disappears the whole is affected.

Below
Like a starry sky, Indra's Net, with the jewels reflected in each other, is a powerful symbol of interdependence.

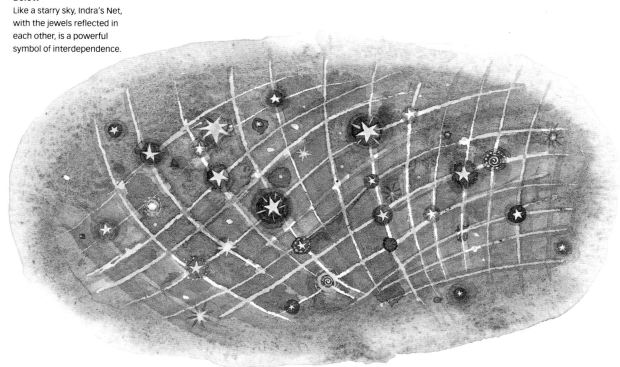

The Twelve Links of Dependent Origination

If we return to the Wheel of Life and look at the outermost circle, we see there are twelve links of dependent origination symbolically represented. They are (starting at the top, going clockwise):

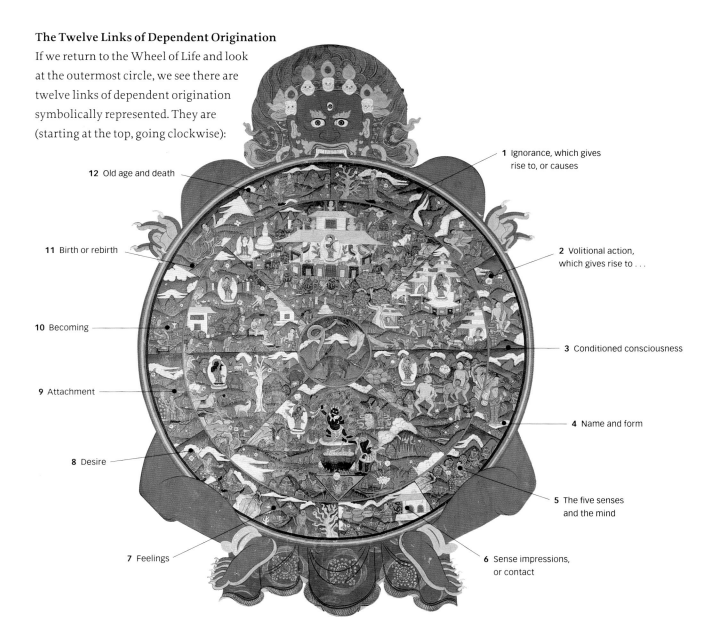

12 Old age and death

11 Birth or rebirth

10 Becoming

9 Attachment

8 Desire

7 Feelings

1 Ignorance, which gives rise to, or causes

2 Volitional action, which gives rise to . . .

3 Conditioned consciousness

4 Name and form

5 The five senses and the mind

6 Sense impressions, or contact

We can see these operating in our lives. For example, in the mistaken belief it will make us happy, we desire a beautiful house that we cannot afford. As a result, we take on an extra job, leaving no time to spend with our partner. Our relationship fails and we turn to drink, which eventually gives us liver cancer and a premature death. This creates the cause for a rebirth with similar conditions, until we learn the lesson and break free from this cycle of suffering. This might appear a little difficult to follow but we have an old saying in our own Western culture that neatly sums up the idea of dependent origination: "One thing leads to another."

The principle of interdependence is fundamental to Buddhism. The reason it is so important is that it helps us understand why we experience suffering. Once we realize an object we desire depends on causes and conditions to exist, its desirability becomes less. Why this is so becomes much clearer after studying the Buddhist principle of emptiness, which develops out of dependent origination and relates integrally to it.

Emptiness

> " *The self may not be something, but neither is it nothing. It is simply ungraspable, unfindable. I am who I am not because of an essential self hidden away in the core of my being, but because of the unprecedented and unrepeatable matrix of conditions that have formed me.* "
>
> STEPHEN BATCHELOR

Emptiness, or *sunyata*, means the absence of independent inherent existence, the lack of any enduring or self-sustaining essence. This means that all things arise in dependence on causes and conditions, as we saw with karma and interdependence.

Emptiness applies to ourselves as much as to phenomena. However, we must not think we are nothing because we don't exist in the way we think we do. It is useful to consider that we are more of an ongoing process than a solid thing.

Buddhist philosophy differentiates two levels of truth. Conventional Truth is how we see the world and ourselves existing. Ultimate Truth is how things actually exist and how Buddhas see the world. So we do exist – quite obviously – in a conventional sense and it would be foolish to deny it. But from the view of Ultimate Truth, we exist only through dependence on causes and conditions; we have no inherent self-existence.

The Snake and the Rope

The great Tibetan philosopher Je Tsong Khapa gave an analogy. We go to the woodshed to collect fuel. It is dark inside and we peer into the gloom trying to find the wood. Suddenly we see a snake! We are full of fear and want to run away. After a while we see the snake doesn't move, so we think we should investigate. Apprehensively we approach the snake, prepared to run away if it moves. As we go closer we see it is a coiled rope and feel huge relief.

Left
Meditating on emptiness – of our life and objects within it – can be liberating.

When we saw the rope in the gloom, it appeared to our mind as if it were a snake, causing fear. But this was just the imputation of our thought; it had no reality, even though it seemed real. We can see from this that our assessment of the reality of how things exist, when based on our senses, can be mistaken.

We sit on a chair meditating. We hear a bird singing. Where does the sound stop and our hearing begin? We get off the chair and make a cup of tea and then put the cup on the chair. The chair now functions as a table. Is it still a chair?

If we examine things we see they are not as solid as we usually take for granted, but we live under the illusion that things exist in this concrete fashion. Let's look at the chair again. What makes it a chair? If we take a leg away, is it still a chair? The chair could not exist without the tree that produced the wood, nor the carpenter who made it. Are the wood and the carpenter part of the chair?

Right
When we meditate we might see that our perception of reality, if perceived through our senses, is mistaken.

Left
When we realize that every object, e.g., a chair, is a sum of parts that have come together temporarily – that every part of it is related to something else and that it, therefore, has no independent inherent identity – we can begin to understand the concept of emptiness or *sunyata*.

Realizing the emptiness of how we and objects exist is liberating. It lessens our attachment to objects and allows us the freedom to simply be, living outside of the straitjacket of the roles we play. Of course we still need to play these roles, being a mother, a husband, an engineer, but we need not mistake them for who we really are.

The Noble Eightfold Path

The eight points of the path are defined under three categories: wisdom, morality, and meditation. However, all these things need to be cultivated together; they are not designed to be learned in a linear sequence. Wisdom, morality, and meditation enrich and reinforce each other; the sum of them is greater than the individual parts. Wisdom includes Right View or Understanding, and Right Thought; Morality includes Right Speech, Right Action, Right Livelihood, and Right Effort; and Meditation includes Right Mindfulness and Right Concentration.

RIGHT VIEW OR UNDERSTANDING

"Right view is the forerunner of the entire path, the guide for all the other factors" (Bhikkhu Bodhi). When we understand that life is permeated by dissatisfaction and accept there is a way out, we then come to realize that the most useful way to spend our time is in following spiritual instructions, like Buddha's, on how to find liberation. However, we need an experiential understanding, not just an intellectual, theoretical appreciation.

If we have tested Buddha's teachings on suffering and dissatisfaction thoroughly in our own lives and seen them to be true, we become confident that what he taught to escape from suffering will work. Merely taking the teachings on trust is just another form of ignorance or blind faith.

This is why Right View belongs to wisdom. It also incorporates understanding that we are responsible for our own destiny, that only we can change the way we are. We cannot change circumstances or people, but we can change our reactions to them. Right View is the foundation of the spiritual path.

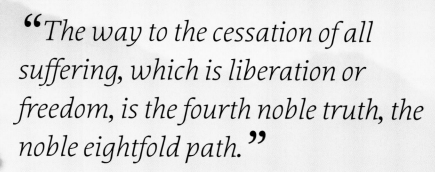

"The way to the cessation of all suffering, which is liberation or freedom, is the fourth noble truth, the noble eightfold path."

AYYA KHEMA

Staying on the Path

Without Right View we can easily get distracted from the path and lose ourselves along the way. Our views and beliefs are fundamental in determining our attitudes and actions, even though we may have only a vague conceptual idea of what these are. Our views shape our perceptions and establish our values, creating a framework through which we interpret the world and the meaning of our existence.

In this way our views condition our actions and inform our choices and efforts to actualize our ideals; they help us decide what to do. Buddha taught that there were two distinct classes of views. If we hold a wrong view, even vaguely, it can lead us to actions that will result in suffering, while holding Right View will steer us towards Right Action and thereby to freedom from suffering.

This is called Mundane Right View but by itself it will only lead to less suffering within cyclic existence. It does not lead to awakening, which is the ultimate purpose of practicing the Buddha's way. So there is another level, called Superior Right View, which realizes the Four Noble Truths, and this leads to a true liberation.

As we saw at the beginning of the Noble Eightfold Path, the different points are not to be seen in a linear progression, and we also work with both levels of Right View at the same time. Though ultimately we are seeking liberation from cyclic existence we also need to make a start, so we develop Right View, which helps us find happiness and avoid suffering in the here and now.

> *"If your intention is wrong, even though you concentrate on emptiness, you will not get a good result because you've been misled. You haven't wisely reflected on things, you haven't let anything go, you're just turning away out of aversion..."*
>
> AJAHN SUMEDHO

RIGHT THOUGHT OR INTENTION

Usually our thoughts are ego-centered and reflect on how best to serve "me." This selfish attitude can be quite subtle and also apply to why we are practicing Buddhism; we want to save only ourselves, or we want to be viewed by others as a great spiritual person, even a guru. So Right Thought includes proper motivation for following Buddha's way.

Right Thought is about changing this habitual and self-centered way of thinking. Then we start to consider others and think more altruistically. We want to practice Buddhism in order to be of benefit to other beings and our environment, not just to make ourselves happy or powerful. At the start we will of course naturally tend to think somewhat selfishly but we can practice changing our motivation.

Buddha explained that Right Thought has three aspects: renunciation, goodwill, and harmlessness. These counter their opposites of desire, ill will, and harmfulness, which arise from a mind that is suffused in ignorance and that has not understood the nature and causes of suffering. The three aspects are beneficial and help us to develop wisdom and eventually lead us to Nirvana. Their opposites lead to harm and suffering for oneself and others and keep us trapped in samsara.

Renunciation, Goodwill, and Harmlessness

An understanding of the Four Noble Truths is important to nurture Right View, and this is also the case with Right Thought. When we realize our life is steeped in suffering our mind turns to renunciation, the abandoning of desire and attachment. If we extend this to encompass all other beings, we realize they too have lives pervaded by suffering and wish to find happiness. This causes thoughts of goodwill to arise, the wish that they find happiness. Reflecting on how all beings suffer inclines us to thoughts of harmlessness, wishing them to be free from suffering.

Buddha said that whatever subject we reflect upon frequently becomes the natural inclination of the mind. So by substituting Right Thought when negative thoughts arise, we can train our mind. This is enhanced by meditation. We can meditate on the suffering inherent in desire to lead our mind toward renunciation. The meditation on lovingkindness is the best remedy for ill will, and the most effective antidote for harmfulness is meditation on compassion.

This keeps our cultivation of Right Thought firmly grounded in practice, so that it is not simply a theoretical exercise. By actively cultivating our motivation to practice for the benefit of all beings, we learn to think less selfishly and more openly. Many formal Buddhist meditation practices begin with developing our motivation to do the meditation for the benefit of all beings and end with dedicating any merit we have generated from doing the practice for the benefit of all beings. In this way, we can develop Right Thought every time we meditate.

RIGHT SPEECH

As with the other steps on the Noble Eightfold Path that come under morality, Right Speech is about being conscious and aware of what we are saying and doing. Morality is not about being judgmental or making us feel unnecessarily guilty. It is about learning how to assess ourselves honestly and being humble when we see we are not perfect, rather than feeling depressed or inadequate.

Right Speech includes everything we say. We might think perhaps that speech is not as important as action but speech – and its development, the written word – can have a big impact, leading to either good or bad consequences. Our modern age has a tremendous capacity and range of verbal expression, so it is more important than ever that we practice Right Speech.

Right Speech has four elements. The first is abstaining from false speech, or lying, and cultivating truthful speech. Always being truthful helps accord with reality and dispels illusion. The second is abstaining from slanderous speech and cultivating speech that promotes friendship and harmony. This arises from and helps develop lovingkindness. The third is abstaining from harsh speech, shouting, insulting, or being sarcastic, and cultivating courteous, friendly speech. This relies on patience and tolerance. The fourth is abstaining from idle chatter, including television, radio, and newspapers, and cultivating speech that is important and valuable. This is supported by mindfulness – not letting our attention be distracted by sensationalism.

> *"If you know anything that's hurtful and untrue, don't say it. If you know anything that's helpful and untrue, don't say it. If you know anything that's hurtful and true, don't say it. If you know anything that's helpful and true, find the right time."*

SHAKYAMUNI BUDDHA

Lies are Lies

We try not to tell lies, though this is difficult in a society where advertising has turned falsehood into an art form. But often we tell little lies to make ourselves appear cleverer or bolder than we really are. These are lies even though we call them exaggeration or omitting the less attractive parts of our story.

Sometimes we tell lies to protect the feelings of others, and this is tricky. If we are conscious of what we are doing, if our motivation is to avoid hurting someone, and if we have thoroughly considered the consequences, then telling the lie may be justified. Telling the truth if possible is, however, the best course of action.

We also try not to use harsh words, shout at others, or upset them. This includes slander, telling stories behind people's backs, and swearing. Using speech in this way is a form of attacking others. It is best to avoid retaliation if someone shouts at us and not shout back in anger or because we feel hurt.

Idle gossip or frivolous speech is time-wasting, unproductive, and can lead to hurting others. Of course we talk about people we know in general conversation, but we can try to find good things to say about others, or just be quiet if someone is criticizing another person. We all know the game of Chinese Whispers, where a sentence is whispered round a group of people and ends up being nothing like the original. Idle gossip is like this but can be much more damaging than a parlor game.

"*Right Action can be done under any circumstances by anyone at any time, be it in the household or at work or in a monastic situation.*"

AYYA KHEMA

RIGHT ACTION

Right Action is about behaving consciously in ways that do not hurt others. Some lay Buddhists like to observe five precepts as their commitment to the Buddhist path; monks and nuns observe many more. We don't have to follow these precepts rigidly but being guided by the principles behind them is conducive to Right Action.

The five precepts are: not killing, not taking that which is not given, not misusing the senses, not lying (covered by Right Speech), and not misusing intoxicants. Not killing seems easy, but if we extend this to all beings we see that it can be difficult. There are many insects we crush simply by walking, but by walking mindfully we can avoid many more than if we walk carelessly. We might think, "Oh, it's only an insect," but Buddha said all beings have buddhanature and like us have the right to try to find happiness.

Abstention from taking life includes suicide, and even if someone feels desperate this precious human rebirth should not be thrown away lightly. We can remind such a person that the feelings behind the wish to take one's own life will change. Torturing and harming other beings are included as secondary actions in not killing. Meditation on kindness and compassion to all beings reinforces this precept..

Stealing, or taking that which is not given, also seems pretty easy, but how many of us have been tempted to keep the extra change given in error by a shopkeeper? Or found a scarf or umbrella on the bus and kept it rather than turning it in? Abstention from taking what is not given also includes fraud and deception.

Being Happy with What We Have

Not stealing is reinforced by always being mindful of our actions, and we can cultivate honesty and respect for the possessions of others. This is reinforced by being satisfied with what we already have and not continuously craving new things. We can also practice generosity and give a little of our own money and possessions to those in need.

Not misusing the senses is difficult in our modern world, which encourages sensual over-indulgence. This includes not overeating, not overindulging in beautiful sights and sounds, and appropriate sexual behavior. Moderation in sex often means we appreciate and respect our partner more, not taking him or her for granted.

Appropriate sexual behavior also means not committing adultery or hurting another person through sex. Practicing sexual fidelity because we love our partner is ultimately more rewarding than promiscuity, which usually causes harm. We can contemplate the fact that monks and nuns practice celibacy.

Some people interpret not misusing intoxicants as abstention, which keeps it simple. However, moderate social use of intoxicants for relaxation rather than intoxication suits some people better. The main reason that Buddha taught abstention from drink and drugs was because they dull the mind, and we tend to use them for escapism. Perhaps the most important reason to refrain from intoxicants or keep our intake moderate is to prevent bad behavior that damages ourselves or others, causing suffering, and that later leads to regrets.

"Treading the path of awakening can embrace a range of purposes. At times we may concentrate on the specifics of material existence: creating a livelihood that is in accord with our deepest values and aspirations. At times we may retreat: disentangling ourselves from social and psychological pressures in order to reconsider our life in a quiet and supportive setting. At times we may engage with the world: responding empathetically and creatively to the anguish of others."

STEPHEN BATCHELOR

RIGHT LIVELIHOOD

Right Livelihood has become much more difficult since the time of the Buddha. It has always been based on the Indian principle of *ahimsa*, or harmlessness, which means making a living in an ethical way. Unfortunately modern society is more interested in profit margins than ethics, so many jobs do not fulfill the principle of harmlessness. Insurance companies, for example, spend a lot of time trying to invalidate people's claims to avoid paying out, which always causes suffering since people assume they are covered.

Monks and nuns traditionally do not work for money, and in the Theravada tradition monastics never actually touch or handle money at all. They live in dependence on alms provided by their lay supporters, who in turn are given spiritual guidance by the monastics. Nuns and monks devote their time to spiritual practice and are therefore deemed worthy of support. In this way they can be said to practice the pinnacle of Right Livelihood.

Choosing a Career

Nonetheless, some of us need to work, some of the time at least! We can try to choose a career that helps people, like being a doctor, nurse, or social worker. As the quotation says, this is responding to the suffering and anguish of others and is of great benefit. However, these jobs can be very demanding and do not suit all dispositions.

We can at least avoid certain jobs, such as being an arms dealer, or working in industries that pollute us (such as the tobacco industry) or the environment. Buddha indicated that any job that brought harm should be avoided. Many jobs seem harmless enough, like being a clerk or a secretary, but we need to look at what the company we work for trades in and avoid companies that cause harm to people, animals, or the environment.

We might wonder why our job is so important to our Buddhist practice. However, we spend a lot of time at work, and inevitably we will be influenced by what we do. So it might cause us some discomfort in our meditations if we reflect that what we do is damaging to others. Buddha taught that our wealth should be acquired according to certain standards: our work must be legal, non-violent, honest, and not cause harm to others.

We can use these principles to assess our current job and help us decide what career or type of work we would like to do. Making large amounts of money is not the only criterion for work. Even though modern society has elevated material well-being above social conscience, we can never be happy if our job causes suffering or is unethical. Overworking is unhealthy and holidays and meditation retreats, if we choose, are important too.

RIGHT EFFORT

Right Effort includes the Buddhist middle way of not trying too hard or too little. If we put all our energy into striving for awareness, we are likely to become too tired to do it all, or be disappointed when we don't succeed quickly. If we don't try hard enough, then nothing much will happen, and we have merely wasted our time.

Right Effort involves energy, which is neutral, but manifests in either positive or negative forms. We see that aggression and desire are fueled by energy, as are generosity and mindfulness. So we try to ensure our energy is directed to wholesome states of mind. But, on its own, good energy will lead only to less suffering, not toward enlightenment. So we cultivate Right Effort alongside Right View, Right Intention, and so forth, in order to awaken to our true nature.

Buddha stressed the importance of Right Effort, the need for diligence, exertion, and perseverance. He showed us that there is a path to liberation but that the rest is up to us. Enlightenment is hard to attain and therefore putting the path into practice requires a lot of work. No one else can do it for us, not our teacher or guru, not even Buddha himself. Our destiny is our own responsibility.

> *"Proper effort is not the effort to make something particular happen. It is the effort to be aware and awake in each moment, the effort to overcome laziness and defilements, the effort to make each activity of our day meditation."*
>
> AJAHN CHAH

Four Great Endeavors

The Buddhist texts describe four aspects of Right Effort called the Four Great Endeavors. The first, preventing unwholesome states of mind from arising, is overcoming defiled states of mind. These are the five hindrances we looked at earlier: sensual desire, ill will, dullness, worry, and doubt. The first two are strongest, but they all hinder concentration, preventing our mind from becoming calm and clear. The best way to prevent any of them from arising is to practice mindfulness.

Despite our best efforts some negative states of mind will still arise. So the second aspect, abandoning unwholesome states of mind already arisen, requires a different effort involving five techniques. The first is substituting a positive thought analogous to the negative thought, so if we feel ill will toward someone, we can turn our mind toward lovingkindness. The second is cultivating shame. The third is redirecting our attention elsewhere, and the fourth, its opposite, is confronting the negative thought. The fifth, only to be used if the others fail, is suppressing the negative thought.

The third aspect of Right Effort is developing positive states of mind not yet arisen. To assist us are Seven Enlightenment Factors: mindfulness, investigation of phenomena, energy, rapture, tranquility, concentration, and equanimity. These are cultivated in turn, and each preceding factor helps the next one. For example, as energy increases, rapture – a pleasurable interest – naturally develops.

The final aspect is maintaining wholesome states of mind once they have arisen. This is achieved by stabilizing and strengthening the Seven Enlightenment Factors. When they are strong they help mature our positive thoughts, ultimately leading to liberation.

"*The task of Right Mindfulness is to clear up the cognitive field. Mindfulness brings to light experience in its pure immediacy. It reveals the object as it is before it has been plastered over with conceptual paint, overlaid with interpretations. To practice mindfulness is thus a matter not so much of doing but of undoing: not thinking, not judging, not associating, not planning, not imagining, not wishing.*"

BHIKKHU BODHI

RIGHT MINDFULNESS

As will become clear in the next chapter, mindfulness is integral to meditation and facilitates the attainment of both serenity, or calm, and insight. We train our mind to remain in the present, simply noting whatever arises as it arises, with no judgment or interpretation. There isn't really an incorrect mindfulness, only its opposite, mindlessness, which is unfortunately how we often spend our lives.

There is a classic analogy where the mind without mindfulness is compared to a pumpkin and the mind established in mindfulness is likened to a stone. A pumpkin placed on water will float, blown in any direction according to the wind and the currents, while a stone sinks directly to the bottom and stays there without deviation. Mindfulness grounds the mind firmly in the present, preventing it floating off into nostalgic memories, hopes, and fears.

On the bus to work we might read a book, but unless we are learning or studying its subject, it often offers only escapism. We are not aware that we are reading and being led along a storyline determined by the author. Of course it is fine to read for relaxation and enjoyment, but we can try to be mindful of what we are doing at the same time. In this way we don't miss our bus stop or feel irritated because we have to stop reading our book to get off the bus.

Four Foundations of Mindfulness

There are traditionally four foundations of mindfulness: mindfulness of the body, of feeling, of thinking, and of the objects of thought. What does this mean for us in our daily lives? Mindfulness of the body is being aware of it as a whole, of its different parts, of breathing, walking, eating, and so on. Often we take our body for granted, so actually becoming aware of it can be quite exciting.

Mindfulness of feeling is one we are all aware of when the feelings are pleasurable or painful, but we tend to get lost in the feeling rather than being mindful of it as a feeling. If we say to ourselves, "This is the painful feeling of having banged my ankle," the awareness of the sensation can help lessen the pain; being mindful rather than reacting.

Mindfulness of thinking is the basis for all meditation. It entails watching our thoughts without becoming involved with them. If we concentrate on how a thought has disturbed us instead of staying disturbed, we are practicing mindfulness of thinking. Similarly, naming our thoughts objectifies them and so helps to let go of them.

"*Right Concentration is found in the meditative absorptions which are mentioned by the Buddha in discourse after discourse as the way and the means, but not as the goal.*"

AYYA KHEMA

RIGHT CONCENTRATION

Without all the other previous steps on the Noble Eightfold Path, Right Concentration cannot arise. In the same way that we need Right View at the beginning to get us on the path, we need all the other steps to help us develop Right Concentration.

Right Concentration is developed by using one of two methods; calm or tranquil abiding meditation and insight meditation. They both require the same preliminary practices. These include pure moral discipline, spiritual guidance from a properly qualified teacher, and living (or at least practicing) in a quiet place conducive to meditation.

Right Concentration develops single-pointedness of mind. This means we learn to stay focused on the subject we have chosen to meditate on. When we can do this, even if just for a few moments, we are not caught up in the usual ego thinking of "I want this," "I don't like that," and so on. However, Right Concentration is developed in stages, it is not attained all at once.

Meditative Absorptions

This practice can lead into states of meditative absorption, which are blissful. Buddha warned that the purpose of meditation is not just to bliss out in these states of mind, but to use them to attain enlightenment. Thus Right Concentration includes meditating with proper motivation, which is the wish to awaken.

The stages of meditative absorption are divided into eight levels, and each is marked by a greater depth, purity, and subtlety than its predecessors. They can only be attained progressively, the development of the next level being dependent on mastery of the former. They all share two fundamental qualities: unbroken attention on the object of concentration and the resulting tranquility of the mind.

Although Right Concentration lies at the end of the Noble Eightfold Path, it does not accomplish the ultimate goal of awakening alone. We also need the penetrating insight of wisdom to liberate ourselves from suffering. So Right Concentration leads us back to Right View at a higher level, because we realize that the best subject to meditate on is our misperception of ourselves and all phenomena, believing them to exist independently and concretely.

Meditating on the emptiness of our own inherent existence – that we exist in dependence on causes, conditions, and circumstances – lessens our ego attachment . This is the development of wisdom, the remedy for ignorance which is the base for all the other mental afflictions. From this we see that the different factors of the Noble Eightfold Path are interdependent and also work at different levels. So whether we are a beginner or a more experienced Buddhist, there is much we can use from the Noble Eightfold Path on our spiritual journey.

"The higher reaches of the path may seem remote from us in our present position, the demands of practice may appear difficult to fulfill. But even if the heights of realization are now distant, all that we need to reach them lies just beneath our feet. The eight factors of the path are always accessible to us; they are mental components which can be established in the mind simply through determination and effort" (Bhikkhu Bodhi).

The Six Perfections

The Six Perfections are generosity, morality, patience, joyful effort or enthusiastic perseverance, concentration or single-pointedness of mind, and wisdom. Buddha taught them in this order, with the easier practices leading on to the harder. Also the previous practice helps form the basis for the next one. For example, it is hard to practice morality if we are attached to our possessions, and the best antidote to attachment is generosity.

" *The path to enlightenment is twofold: wisdom and skillful means. The practice of the first four perfections is the practice of skillful means. The last two perfections reveal the practice of wisdom.* "

BUDDHA

Below
We give from our hearts to others through our actions, when there is pure motivation in us to be generous.

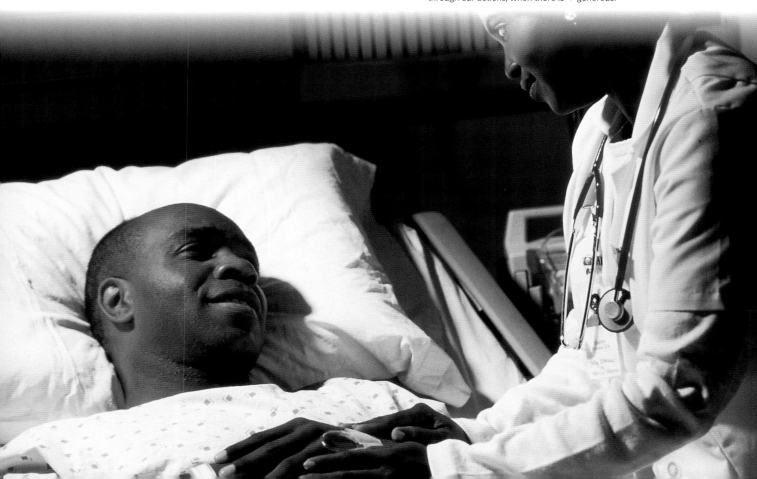

Generosity

Traditionally there are three kinds of generosity: giving material help to those who lack material necessities, giving protection to those in fear, and giving pure, sincere Dharma teachings to those who request them.

Giving material help includes giving to charity, beggars, friends in need, and to famine or disaster victims. Some of these people or organizations are easier to give to than others. We may feel like helping a friend and giving to a particular charity only but if we really think about it, all needy people require assistance, whether we like them or believe in their cause or not. This doesn't mean we should give away all our possessions to everyone who needs them! However, thinking about those who lack the things we have with kindness rather than scorn or blame helps develop generosity. Then we can give skillfully any material assistance we are able to offer. As Geshe Wangchen says: ". . . giving any helpful advice in a sincere way is also the practice of generosity."

Pure Motivation

This leads to our motivation for giving. If we practice generosity to make ourselves look good, this is not pure giving. Or if we throw a few coins at a beggar with disgust in our eyes, this is also not pure giving. We must give from our hearts as well as our pockets for the act of giving to be complete.

We can also be mindful of what we give. Gifts of alcohol, tobacco, or drugs, though they may give some temporary relief, might in the long run be injurious. Similarly, killing one animal to feed another, like giving a live fish to a seagull, is also inappropriate. Considering what we give is as important as how we give it.

There are many opportunities to give protection to those in fear in our modern world. It is unfortunately quite common for people to be robbed or attacked, and doing what we can to help these individuals is real generosity. Similarly, there are charities to help torture victims, street children, and maltreated animals. Supporting organizations like these helps provide much relief.

We might think giving Dharma teachings is well beyond our capability, particularly if we have only recently encountered Buddhism. In some ways this is correct, but the essence of what Buddha taught is simple kindness and compassion toward others, and – if we are asked to say something – we can all mention these qualities. The Dalai Lama has often been heard to say, "My religion is kindness."

The Six Perfections

"*I agree that it is tough to be moral in today's world, where people do indeed seem to be rewarded for stealing. It comes down to practice. There are two kinds of people; those who practice and those who don't. And what is your reward? The proverb says 'Virtue is its own reward,' which is more enjoyable than it sounds.*"

ROBERT AITKEN

Below
True morality is refraining from negative actions of body, speech, and mind, while also cultivating good qualities like love and compassion, and practicing kindness to everyone.

MORALITY

Practicing morality is mindfully refraining from any negative actions. Traditionally these are classified as the Ten Nonvirtues. There are four nonvirtues of speech: telling lies, slandering others, gossiping, and using harsh words and swearing. There are three non-virtues of body: killing, stealing, and sexual misconduct; and three of mind: craving and attachment, wishing to harm others, and holding wrong views.

By sincerely trying to avoid negative behavior, our mind becomes calm and clear, so we feel happy. We have all experienced how angry and troubled we feel if we have harmed someone, even if we feel justified, or satisfied and happy when we have actually helped someone, even in a small way.

Morality includes cultivating good qualities too, not just avoiding negative behavior. So we try to develop love, kindness, and compassion for others, as well as not harming them. This is quite easy to do for our friends and family but if we think about how everybody wants to be happy and avoid suffering equally, then we can try to expand our goodwill toward all beings.

Buddha taught that morality is the foundation of a single-pointed mind. We can see this from the literal translation of *shila* – morality – which means cool and peaceful. When our mind is free from negative emotions it becomes tranquil and focused, and then positive mind states, such as love and compassion, arise naturally.

Cultivating Morality

However, practicing morality is not always easy! So we can try to engender morality in our meditation sessions. Many meditations are designed to help us in this way. But we must also try to practice morality in everyday life too, otherwise it remains theoretical.

It is important to remember Buddha's middle way. We have probably all met people who – despite their best intentions – seem overly pious and rigid. So we must be careful not to reduce morality to a set of inflexible rules regardless of circumstances.

It is somewhat unlikely that we can practice pure morality in all things at the beginning of our practice. So we keep a perspective on morality by understanding that some actions have more serious consequences than others. However, it is important not to repress our negative emotions. If we feel angry toward someone we can refrain from expressing it to the person, instead finding a sympathetic friend and telling him or her about it. This will allow us to exorcise the negative feelings in a nonharmful way.

The Six Perfections

" *Impatience is almost invariably the ego's response to adverse experiences or suffering, or indeed to anything that frustrates the fulfillment of its projects and programs. Its contrary, therefore, patience, represents a will to accept and bear conditions that may be painful, unpleasant, or simply not in conformity with what one wants.* "

JOHN SNELLING

Below
Farmers must develop patience as they bear crop-growing problems and uncomfortable harvesting situations in their attempts to survive.

PATIENCE

Practicing patience gives us great inner strength and courage to face difficult situations. It helps us discover the real cause of problems and not to simply react by blaming temporary circumstances. If we are patient, we are less likely to get upset quickly when things don't go our way and less likely to act badly toward others.

Traditionally patience is classified into three types: the patience of forgiveness, the patience of accepting suffering, and the patience of being able to behave virtuously.

The nature of our world is inherently unsatisfactory, so troublesome situations will definitely arise. So, when someone gets angry with us, or abuses us, we also naturally tend to be angry and abusive toward the person. This merely aggravates the situation. If we practice patience instead of mindlessly reacting, we realize the person is suffering and out of control. However, we do not have to behave in the same way. If we stay calm, eventually the person's anger will lessen and the situation can be resolved calmly.

Accepting Suffering

The patience of accepting suffering is of great use in our lives, because suffering will inevitably arise due to the unsatisfactory nature of our existence. Normally when we suffer and face problems and difficulties we think of them as really bad. If we accept the situation with patience and remind ourselves that even this too will pass, then we lessen the experience of suffering.

The Japanese poet Issa accepted the presence of fleas and lice as part of his daily life. But he transformed his irritation through cultivating patience to the point where he treated them as friends. In this Haiku poem he is talking to the fleas that lived on his body as he prepared to go on a trip:

Now you fleas!
You shall see Matsushima –
Off we go!

Patience can help us transform how we think about our problems. If we regard them as teachers, providing us with the opportunity to learn, we are less distressed when they arise. We cannot prevent problems – this is the nature of life – but transforming how we think about them helps us deal with them more successfully.

The Six Perfections

" *Dharma practice is founded on resolve. This is not an emotional conversion, a devastating realization of the error of our ways, a desperate urge to be good, but an ongoing, heartfelt reflection on priorities, values, and purpose. We need to keep taking stock of our life in an unsentimental, uncompromising way.* "

STEPHEN BATCHELOR

Below
Joyful effort stems from the resolve to complete actions one believes to have merit with a positive state of mind and confidence, by patiently encouraging ourselves despite any setbacks.

JOYFUL EFFORT

Following the Buddha's path is rewarding but not always easy, and changing our old habitual patterns and learning new ways of being is an ongoing process. There is little point in giving up when the going gets tough, as these are moments of greatest opportunity. So this is where joyful effort, or enthusiastic perseverance, comes in.

Joyful effort incorporates our attitude toward our spiritual practice. If our attitude is only to follow a set of rules rigidly and blindly, then we are probably quite miserable! If, however, we remind ourselves thoroughly of the great benefit to ourselves and others from practicing what Buddha taught, this helps us cultivate joyful effort. Then we approach the Buddhist path with great joy at having found such a wonderful way of life.

Joyful effort includes great determination to keep practicing, even when we are depressed or facing problems. It encourages us to keep trying and helps us maintain our resolve when we feel weak. Joyful effort is also the best antidote to laziness, not just when we are meditating, but in all activities of our daily life.

Three Aspects of Joyful Effort

Traditionally, joyful effort has three aspects. The first is understanding the great value in practicing a spiritual path and developing confidence that we can do it. If we come to Buddhism feeling helpless and inadequate, then our attitude is too passive. We think that meditation and Buddhist practice will take care of us, that we don't have to do anything other than sit on a meditation cushion. So we develop joyful effort by reminding ourselves often of the great virtues of Dharma practice. This gives us the strength to follow Buddha's way.

The second aspect is maintaining joyful effort despite all the setbacks we encounter. Buddhist practice is a continual process, not something we do once a day or a few times a week. So we must have great determination not to give up. We can resolve not to lose strength and maintain joyful effort by meditating on the many benefits of Dharma practice.

We develop and maintain our Dharma practice, but we still need some extra impetus. This is the third aspect of joyful effort, the encouragement to follow our practice through. In practical terms this means not giving up watching our breath after five minutes and staying patient in the traffic jam until it clears. We can remind ourselves of our innate buddhanature that will one day shine through all our delusions.

The Six Perfections

"*A single-pointed mind (Sanskrit samatha) is the fully trained state of the meditative mind. It serves as the ground for cultivating wisdom (Sanskrit prajna), which is the ultimate antidote to our delusions.*"

GESHE WANGCHEN

Below

If we live in a peaceful place conducive to meditation, accept what comes our way without craving other things, maintain morality, and drop pointless activity, this will help develop concentration and enable painstaking work such as carpet weaving.

CONCENTRATION OR SINGLE-POINTED MIND

The last two perfections come under wisdom, because without concentration we cannot penetrate deeply into an object of meditation and thereby realize its true nature. Without developing single-pointedness of mind, our meditation will not realize its full potential. This is based on developing virtuous qualities of mind and eliminating deluded states of mind. We should first practice mindfulness meditation, which is explained with instructions in the next chapter. This calms the mind and improves our concentration. When our mind is calm, we can focus our attention on an object. Once we are able to analyze the nature of the object, we can realize the truth of how it actually exists. We can meditate on a physical object such as a statue of Buddha, or a nonphysical object such as the luminosity of our own mind. The latter refers to the mind freed from thoughts, emotions, and ego preoccupations. When we begin, our mind will frequently wander away from the object, and we need to keep bringing our attention back. We can practice mindfulness of breathing until the mind calms down. The other main distraction is dullness, when the mind becomes tired and sleepy. We can lift the mind by reflecting on the excellent qualities of Buddha.

Three Stages of Single-Pointed Mind

Buddha explained how to develop a single-pointed mind in three stages. The first, the six prerequisites, are the base upon which we develop single-pointed mind. These are: living in a safe, quiet environment conducive to meditation and close to our spiritual guide; controlling desire by meditating on impermanence and the unsatisfactory nature of our lives; being contented with our lives, not craving what we don't have; renouncing meaningless activities; maintaining morality; and avoiding discursive thought, when our mind drifts aimlessly. The second stage is the actual practice of single-pointed mind which has three points: meditating in the correct posture, described in the next chapter; using an object of meditation to develop concentration, which can be a physical object or a subject we contemplate mentally; and developing concentration by avoiding wandering thoughts from an overstimulated mind and mental dullness from a sleepy or tired mind. The result of practicing single-pointed mind is the third stage and has two major benefits. These are alertness and suppleness of mind and pacification of mental obstacles, which leads to stability and clarity of mind.

The Six Perfections

"*The Superior Avalokiteshvara, the bodhisattva, the great being, replied to the Venerable Shariputra as follows: 'Shariputra, whatever son or daughter of the lineage wishes to engage in the practice of the profound perfection of wisdom should look perfectly like this … Form is empty; emptiness is form. Emptiness is not other than form; form is also not other than emptiness.'*"

SHAKYAMUNI BUDDHA

Below
Like the two wings of an eagle, skillful means and wisdom help us fly toward enlightenment.

WISDOM

In these famous words from the Heart Sutra, Buddha teaches the essence of the perfection of wisdom; form and emptiness are not essentially different. At first glance this might seem contradictory and difficult to understand. What does it actually mean? We experience forms or objects as solid entities. We have read that emptiness means they exist in dependence on their constituent parts, causes, and conditions.

But emptiness is also empty; it cannot exist by itself and is dependent on causes and conditions, too – such as someone realizing its true nature. There is no solid ground to stand upon. Yet it is our tendency to try to hold on to things as solid entities, solid beliefs. There are simply objects and our perception of these forms, which differ subtly from person to person. It is not a question of my perception being better than yours, or yours being right and mine wrong. They both exist differently simply because each of us is unique; no two people have had exactly the same experiences and reactions to them. And this is where the problems of our world begin and end. If we do not take our own perception of reality too seriously and allow other people to have theirs, then there are fewer rigid viewpoints and fewer arguments.

The Hardest to Realize

This is the last of the Six Perfections, and the hardest to realize. Without generosity, morality, joyful effort, patience, and single-pointed mind, we are unable to practice the perfection of wisdom fully. However, wisdom must also inform the other five perfections. Otherwise self-identity arises, for example, with an act of generosity – "I am being generous," which only leads to the accumulation of merit.

When wisdom informs an act of generosity there is no sense of "I" giving; the act is a spontaneous gesture arising from compassion. When we give – or practice morality, and so on – in this way, such acts lead us toward enlightenment. And this is why we are practicing Buddhism, to be free of the sufferings of cyclic existence.

Traditionally, the simile used to illustrate this point likens this twofold approach to the two wings of a bird. Thus we practice the first five perfections – albeit at the beginning with self-identity – in order to develop wisdom, and we also practice wisdom in order to let go of self-identity with our actions. This is the uniting of method, or skillful means, with wisdom, and when these two things work together in harmony we can fly toward enlightenment.

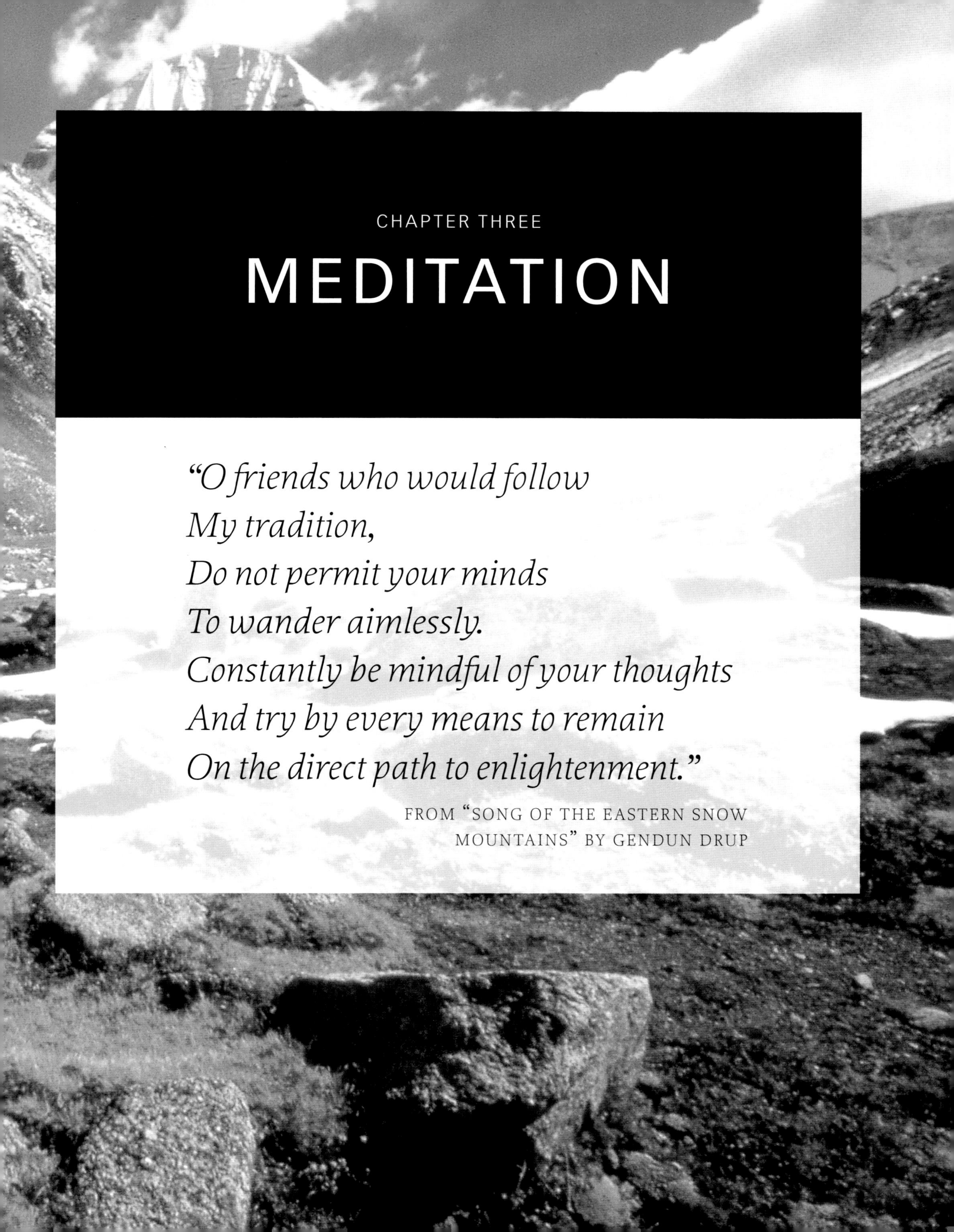

CHAPTER THREE

MEDITATION

"O friends who would follow
My tradition,
Do not permit your minds
To wander aimlessly.
Constantly be mindful of your thoughts
And try by every means to remain
On the direct path to enlightenment."

FROM "SONG OF THE EASTERN SNOW
MOUNTAINS" BY GENDUN DRUP

Meditation is an internal process of discovering and becoming familiar with our mind. By practicing meditation we can develop insight into ourselves: our emotions, thoughts, and feelings. This exploration of mind is the practical aspect of Buddhism and how we realize the truth in the principles we have read in the preceding chapter.

The willingness to remain open to our experience while meditating is important. We tend to believe our view of the world and how things exist to be definitive, but meditation can open our minds to a deeper level of understanding.

We need to resolve firmly to practice regularly. Otherwise our experience will be superficial and we will not gain much benefit. We must also be careful of the other extreme and not overdo it, as we will then tire quickly. A good balance is to meditate every day, or several times a week, but for not longer than ten to fifteen minutes per session in the beginning.

Try not to have too many high expectations. This is difficult, because we hope to find peace and inner wisdom through our meditation, but these goals can become obstacles and close us off to our experience if we expect too much at the beginning. If your mind seems to race more than usual, don't panic! This is natural when we start to meditate.

Above
When you begin meditating, it is not necessarily useful to sit for as long as this Buddhist monk in Sri Lanka does.

Right
A cushion in a clean, simply furnished room in a peaceful setting is good for meditators, although any quiet place is adequate.

Letting Go of Thoughts

1   If painful thoughts or memories arise, simply observe them and let them go. Try not to dwell in past experiences. The same goes for pleasant thoughts, in which we must be mindful not to indulge. All thoughts are impermanent and we can experience this through meditation.

2   It is good to have a purpose for meditating, beyond the desire to find peace. An appropriate Buddhist motivation is the wish to become enlightened. This may sound daunting but even Buddha had to start somewhere! This wish will help sustain us when our meditation is not following our hopes and expectations.

3   The best way to start meditating is to have the support of a meditation teacher and friends who meditate. Even the simple meditations described here can be substantially enriched by the guidance of a teacher and like-minded friends.

Below
When you begin meditating, it is best, at first, to have the encouragement of a teacher and friends who also meditate.

Why Do We Meditate?

Everyone wants to find happiness and avoid suffering. Often we seek happiness in phenomena outside ourselves: beautiful objects, delicious food, a perfect relationship, success, and fame. We think that if we have these things they will bring happiness.

Though these things certainly give pleasure for a time, they cannot give lasting happiness. This is because they are impermanent and will therefore change, as indeed will our own criteria for what makes us happy. We might have noticed that something which made us happy for a while made us miserable later; like when we fall in love but realize later that we no longer have the same feelings.

However, as we read in the last chapter, things do not exist independently; everything exists in dependence on other things, and nothing is intrinsically good or bad. So none of these phenomena can really make us happy. Understanding this through meditation and realizing we can change our perception of and relationship to these things, helps us alleviate suffering and find happiness.

Above

On retreat in Scotland a monk hangs out his washing. It is advisable to ask for advice from a | spiritual teacher who knows you well before undertaking a retreat to deepen meditation practices.

We also meditate in response to existential dilemmas. "Meditation does not add anything to life; it recovers what has been lost. It is a growing awareness of what our existence is saying to us and asking of us ... Meditation and mystery are inseparable" (Stephen Batchelor). This inquiring into the meaning of life helps us allow happiness and suffering to exist, without craving the former and trying to avoid the latter.

Left

Nuns in Thailand also strive to become awake like the Buddha, although their perception perhaps differs slightly from that of Zen practitioners about what it means to be truly awake – in both heart and mind.

Time and Place

1   When we decide to start meditating we need to find a conducive time and place. It is sensible to practice often. Meditation then becomes a regular habit integrated into our life so we derive the greatest benefit from it.

2   A fundamental requirement is privacy. We don't want people to interrupt us and ask us what we are doing. Though we have decided to meditate, other people might find this strange or silly. If we keep our practice personal this avoids any unnecessary problems.

3   A quiet private room is ideal, but this is not always possible. Simply select the best place you can. The time you choose can help in gaining peace and quiet. Early in the morning is a good time as the mind is clear, not yet distracted by the activities of the coming day. Getting up 15 minutes earlier than usual will give you enough time for a meditation session.

4   Another good time is last thing at night, when the day's activities are finished. However, we may find our mind is tired and we have to watch out for not falling asleep during our meditation session! But if our mind is troubled by something that happened in the day, this is a good opportunity to let it go and become quiet before going to sleep.

5   It is sensible to experiment with times and places. Once you have found your optimum situation, try to be consistent. In time you will find that just going to your room at the normal time is a wonderful refuge from the busyness of life.

Posture

Correct posture is important because mind and body rely on each other. If we are uncomfortable, our minds will become distracted. So developing a good posture at the beginning of meditation is helpful.

The classic posture used by Buddhist meditators is sitting with crossed legs on a meditation cushion. The legs can be crossed with the right leg in front in full lotus – called vajrasana posture – or in half lotus, or simply resting comfortably on the floor. The cushion is positioned to support the back balanced on the pelvis, with the legs in front.

However, sitting on the floor is not always comfortable and is not essential. An alternative is sitting on a chair or meditation stool. Most important is keeping the back straight. This allows our energy to flow freely and – though it may be a little difficult at first – it helps us to meditate comfortably.

When you first begin to meditate, try out the different positions. You can alternate different postures, or stay with the one that you find most comfortable.

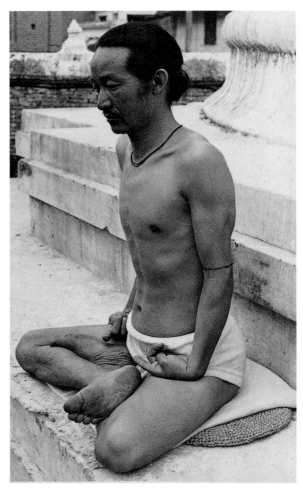

Above
The posture of this Tibetan tantric yogi is highly specialized and relates to his tantric practice. It is important not to attempt it without preparation and instruction from a teacher.

Left
Variations on the traditional meditation posture are illustrated here as modern Westerners normally do not have the physical agility to accomplish it easily. Most important is to keep the back straight and to remain comfortable enough to breathe calmly and easily.

The Correct Posture

1 Sit with the head inclined slightly forward and eyes loosely shut or partly open and looking down. This helps prevent both distractions and sleepiness.

2 Arms are gently folded and resting in your lap, palms upward, with one hand on top of the other.

3 The whole posture should be relaxed and free from tension. This helps the mind to be clear and calm.

4 Inevitably, some discomfort will arise from sitting still. We should try to find a balance between fidgeting and being in pain. This is best achieved by simply allowing ourselves to notice when discomfort arises, but not reacting immediately. Explore the sensation for a while. You may notice the discomfort passes naturally. If it does not, or if it increases, then gently shift your position.

Above
If sitting on the floor is uncomfortable, a meditation stool can be used.

Left
The most important element of the meditation posture is the straightness of the back.

Tranquil Abiding or Calm Meditation

> *"Having understood that only wisdom, which is firmly grounded on single-pointed mind, enables us to eliminate delusions from their root, we should first seek to develop single-pointed mind as the base of wisdom."*

SHAKYAMUNI BUDDHA

Left
This statue of Chenrezig, the Tibetan bodhisattva of compassion, is shown here at Samye Monastery, Tibet. The state of selfless love and compassion that Chenrezig symbolizes acts as an inspiration for practicing meditation.

C alm meditation is traditionally known as *samatha*, or tranquil abiding. This means calming and stabilizing the mind to develop concentration, which leads to the single-pointed mind in the quotation. This meditation is the basis of all meditations, as without calm concentration we cannot gain control over our mind. Therefore we can practice tranquil abiding meditation on its own, or as the preliminary practice for any other meditation. It is the best meditation for beginners but useful for experienced meditators, too.

Below
Calm meditation is known as *samatha* and is the basis of all meditational forms, as it stabilizes the mind for concentration.

Calm Meditation Practice

1   Sit quietly in the meditation posture.

2   Become aware of being in the present, here and now, and relax into this space.

3   Resolve to let go of your thoughts, fantasies about the future, nostalgia about the past, mulling over problems, etc.

4   Maintain a balance between trying too hard and becoming sleepy and dull.

5   Bring your attention to your breathing and notice the sensation at the tip of your nostrils for each breath in and out.

6   You might find it useful to count each complete breath up to ten, starting again when you reach the end or your mind wanders, but this is optional.

7   Be careful only to watch the breath and do not try to make it deeper or different in any way.

8   Each time you notice your mind has strayed from the breath and followed some thought, gently bring your attention back to your breathing.

9   Be aware that your mind will probably wander a lot and do not be too critical of yourself, but do not become lazy and indulge in your thoughts and fantasies, either.

Right
When practicing calm meditation, it is important to concentrate on each breath.

Insight Meditation

> *" Through vipassana [insight] meditation, the mind arrives at the understanding that 'everything that arises passes away and is not self' — which is what buddhas know. "*
>
> JOHN SNELLING

Above
This monk, perched on a stone bench, is meditating in the classic meditation posture.

Left
An eleventh-century bronze bodhisattva seated in vajrasana, or "diamond posture."

Insight meditation, known traditionally as *vipassana*, uses the mind to inquire deeply into all phenomena that arise in the mind. This means looking penetratively at our feelings and thoughts, and analyzing them.

Through this meditation we eventually discover that all we encounter in our mind is unsatisfactory, impermanent, and not our true self. This is quite different from how our mind habitually identifies with thoughts and feelings.

This open confrontation with the contents of our mind often brings up old repressed memories which can be disturbing or painful for us. By simply allowing them to rest in consciousness, not judging or being afraid of them, we can observe their insubstantial nature. The person who experienced your painful memories is no longer you, and you do not have to identify with past feelings. In this way, our greatest fears and pains no longer have the same intensity.

Insight Meditation Practice

1 Sit quietly in the meditation posture.

2 Spend a few minutes calming your mind with mindfulness meditation.

3 Watch your thoughts and feelings as they arise and pass.

4 Bring your attention to whatever arises and focus firmly on it.

5 Deepen the focus and start to analyze your thoughts and feelings. Be careful not to identify with them – they are not your true self. Keep your inquiry steady.

6 If you become distracted or upset, bring your attention back to the breath and spend a few minutes doing mindfulness meditation until your mind is calm again.

7 Be aware that even your most traumatic memories are insubstantial; they too simply arise and pass away.

8 It is a good idea to alternate between mindfulness and insight meditation practices; they reinforce each other and protect the mind from becoming too agitated or too dull.

Left
Insight meditation helps deepen the focus on thoughts and feelings.

Walking Meditation

"One walks in file, very slowly, silently, with eyes lowered. . . . Mindfulness is maintained while walking, taking one step with the left foot while breathing in, and one step with the right foot while breathing out."

THICH NHAT HANH

Sitting meditation is often alternated with walking meditation, though one usually sits more than walks. As with the other meditations, maintaining awareness is important. There is the added benefit of easing any pain or stiffness that may have occurred while sitting.

The experience is distinct from sitting because the body is moving. Usually we take walking for granted and are largely unconcerned with what we are doing or how we are doing it. We are more interested in getting from one place to another. In walking meditation, the walking itself is the object: we are not going anywhere.

In walking meditation we walk in a straight line for a distance of about twenty meters, pause, then turn, and retrace our steps. This is repeated for the duration of our walking meditation. Practicing walking meditation in nature can enrich the experience, as long as we do not become distracted.

Below
Maintaining awareness is of ultimate importance in any meditative practice, whether undertaken indoors or outdoors. Buddha statues carved from stone, like this one in Kathmandu, Nepal, are found in outdoor environments all over the East and are used as objects of meditative focus and reminders to people to be aware.

Walking Meditation Practice

1 Stand for a few minutes and calm the mind with mindfulness meditation.

2 Start to walk slowly and rhythmically.

3 Develop awareness of all areas of your body.

4 Be conscious of each lifting and putting down of your feet. You can do this in time with your breathing, as Thich Nhat Hanh suggests opposite.

5 When you reach the turning place, pause, and become aware of simply standing.

6 Turn slowly and walk again.

7 If you become distracted, stand for a few moments in mindfulness meditation. When your attention returns, start to walk again.

Right
Slow, regular walking will calm the mind and develop awareness of your body.

Maintaining Mindfulness

" *Mindfulness is essential for successful meditation; and in our day-to-day lives it keeps us centered, alert, and conscientious, helping us to know what is happening in our mind as it happens and thus to deal skillfully with problems as they arise.* "

KATHLEEN MCDONALD

Mindfulness is concerned with knowing the process of thinking in addition to our thoughts and is traditionally called *Satipatthanna*. As well as the tranquil abiding meditation already described, we can learn to practice mindfulness in everyday life. A simple technique is to watch thoughts as they arise and instead of following a particular thought, give it a label and then decide to let it go.

This is mindfulness in action. It can help us not to get drawn into negative situations. If, for example, you are worrying about something, usually the mind becomes fixated on the issue, often to the exclusion of whatever else is happening around you. Instead of this, you can label the thought "worry" and consciously not indulge it.

In this way it ceases to have such a powerful hold over the mind. It also allows us to be aware of life around us. Of course, the thought will probably arise again in a few moments! But if we continue to label and let go, eventually we will gain some control over our mind.

Below and Right
Mindful meditation entails not following any particular thought, watching it appear like lightning and then fade away in the mind without elaborating upon it – the object being to develop choiceless awareness of how the mind operates.

The Benefits of Mindfulness

1   If we practice mindfulness, we will begin to gain some distance from our thoughts. This standing back allows us to notice that we have habitual thought patterns as certain thoughts and reactions arise regularly.

2   We might observe that we tend to be pessimistic. This might be quite a shock; often when we start meditating and practicing mindfulness we see a less idealized aspect of ourselves. This does not mean we are worse than we thought, simply that we had not noticed before!

3   By seeing our thought patterns just as thoughts that arise and pass, and realizing they are not integral to ourselves, we have a chance to change them. This is unlikely to happen quickly. We have probably spent our lives up until now following our thoughts uncritically and developing habitual ways of thinking. So it will take time and effort to change this.

   We can see practicing mindfulness as training our mind. It takes years of hard study to be a doctor, but if this is what we want, we are happy to undertake it. The benefits of practicing mindfulness are immeasurable; we can wake up from our usual daydreams and live more in the present.

Left
Mindfulness will enable thought patterns to be observed and changed – although this will take time.

Informal Meditation

Above
Meditation does not have to be
practiced in a particular place. The
same awareness may be experienced while one is gardening.

Below
We can practice mindfulness
anywhere. Becoming aware of
any situation and one's place
within it is useful.

"*The practice of
mindfulness … should be
brought to bear on what
is happening at any and
every moment.*"

JOHN SNELLING

Often when we think of meditation, the
image arises of an ancient Eastern sage
sitting in a cave. Such people have the opportunity
and desire to dedicate their lives to meditation.
However, most of us wish to maintain our family
commitments, careers, and hobbies. So we need to
discover how to bring the qualities of our meditations into our daily lives.

Often we are frustrated with delays, such as
waiting for a bus or for the traffic lights to change.
These are excellent situations for informal meditation. Usually we become impatient, wanting to get a
move on and be elsewhere. Yet these moments are as
much a part of our lives as more enjoyable times. If
we habitually feel angry in these situations we are
wasting this part of life, wishing it away. Life is short
– as an encounter with death will reveal – so these
moments are precious too.

How do we meditate in public situations without
other people thinking we are weird? Obviously we
cannot sit cross-legged and shut-eyed! But we can
remember we are breathing and focus our attention
on the breath. Thich Nhat Hanh suggests that we
can thank these situations as opportunities for
informal breathing meditation.

Labeling Our Feelings

1 We can also be mindful of what is happening, and by labeling our feelings "frustration" or "anger," we can lessen their impact. By not indulging these negative emotions, we can find some peace of mind. This helps break the habit of getting angry each time we just miss the bus.

2 By looking at the situation dispassionately we can apply reason and common sense. If, for example, the traffic is heavy and making us late, instead of getting increasingly angry and upset we can analyze the situation. We realize it is not our fault, we cannot change the circumstances, and there is no benefit arriving in a bad mood. By seeing the pointlessness of negative emotions, they lose their power over us.

3 We don't need difficult situations to practice informal meditation, we can use many daily life activities as well. We can be mindful in the bath, watch our breathing in bed before sleeping, and analyze our thoughts while walking to the shops. Once we start meditating in this way, our whole life becomes an opportunity to experience the benefits of meditation.

Right
Watching our breathing before sleep is a practice of informal meditation.

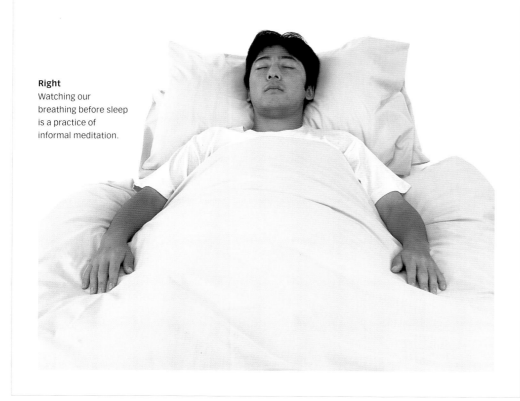

Dealing with Negative Emotions

> "*The only way we can find peace in our own hearts, find the pathway that leads to liberation, is by changing ourselves, not by changing the world.*"
>
> AYYA KHEMA

Left
Nothing is wrong with enjoying food, but overindulgence in sensual desires provokes greed.

In Buddhism there are traditionally five major hindrances or negative mental states. These are:

1. greed
2. anger
3. idleness
4. distraction
5. sceptical doubt

The first two arise frequently and cause more anguish than the others, so we will focus on them. Greed arises from overindulgence in sensual desires.

We all need to eat to survive and there is nothing wrong with choosing food we like and enjoying a good meal. But if eating becomes too important, it turns into greed.

Practicing moderation and restraint is a good antidote to greed. Buddhist monastics generally don't eat after midday – a formal method of restraint or renunciation. Lay Buddhists don't have to be so strict but not overindulging in food is a good place to start, and we can think of the saying: "Eat to live, not live to eat!" It is also an opportunity to think of others and not be selfish; we can offer the last slice of cake to someone else instead of grabbing it for ourselves. In this way, practicing restraint helps cultivate generosity too.

The same attitude helps with other sensual desires, like wanting the person we love to love us, and craving physical and emotional contact. If we truly love the other person we want them to be happy, and they might already be happy without being in a relationship with us. Or we can see that our desire for that person is causing us unhappiness, so there is no point indulging it and we should try to let it go.

Anger

Buddha likened anger to picking up hot coals with our bare hands and throwing them at someone. Both people get hurt, but we get hurt first. Anger generally arises from feeling hurt, and we think that if we reciprocate in kind we will feel better – absurd! It simply causes more pain and anger. We can reflect on the old Chinese proverb: "If you seek revenge, first dig two graves!" People sometimes think expressing anger to others is good, but how can causing further negative emotions be good?

However, repressing anger without dealing with it is not healthy. The best antidote to anger is lovingkindness, to ourselves and those who caused us anger. Lovingkindness develops from realizing that only someone who is unhappy will hurt someone else. Therefore the person who hurt us cannot be happy, and we should try to feel compassion rather than anger toward them.

Below
Buddha compared the expression of anger to picking up hot coals and hurling them at someone.

Temple Etiquette

Above

It is customary to remove one's shoes before entering a Buddhist temple or shrine room, as a mark of respect.

I f you have never been to a Buddhist temple or shrine room, the experience might seem a little strange. Our modern world is full of places dedicated to entertainment, but however pleasant they are, they distract us from our inner life. The quiet spaciousness of a Buddhist shrine room can therefore be unfamiliar, so understanding how to behave in these places of spiritual practice is useful.

Going to a Buddhist temple is similar to going into a church, synagogue, or other place of worship. These places are dedicated to spiritual practice, and feelings of reverence and respect arise when we enter them, as the atmosphere seems permeated with religious experience.

Above
Different schools of Buddhism have different kinds of shrine rooms, temples, and meditative practices. Above, Buddhist monks in Thailand are chanting in a simple room.

Temples and Shrine Rooms

The different Buddhist traditions have quite different shrine rooms. A Theravada meditation hall will contain a large statue of Buddha. These are works of art as well as being religious icons, and this is reflected in the style; a Thai Buddha looks different from a Burmese Buddha. Zen temples emphasize simplicity and are quite bare, though there is usually one Buddha image. In contrast, Tibetan shrine rooms, or *gompas*, are colorful and highly decorated with lots of paintings and statues.

Inside these different shrine rooms, our behavior is similar. If we are sensitive to the atmosphere, we tend to speak quietly and thoughtfully, and walk softly. Often there will be a Buddhist teacher present. We behave respectfully toward such people – not just because of who they are but in appreciation of their spiritual qualities. If the teacher is a monk or nun, we need to be mindful of the rules they follow and try not to infringe these. This is particularly important in the Theravada tradition. A monk should not have any physical contact with a woman, not even shaking hands. The same is true for nuns not touching men. A bow with folded hands is the appropriate greeting.

Before going in it is customary to remove one's shoes. Not only is this a mark of respect, it serves the useful function of keeping the floor clean. As it is usual to sit on meditation cushions on floor mats, this is obviously sensible. Wearing clothes that are modest and comfortable for sitting on the floor is also important; miniskirts and skintight jeans are best avoided! Meditation halls are often large and can be draughty, so warm clothes are important too.

Left
A Tibetan refugee's altar in Manali has pictures of the Dalai Lama and images sacred to Tibetan Buddhists, who traditionally pray and practice in front of such altars in their homes.

Right
This temple in Chiang Mai, Thailand, holds large statues of the Buddha and other bodhisattvas.

Prostrations

> *"Reverently I prostrate with my body, speech, and mind, and present clouds of every type of offering, actual and mentally transformed…"*
>
> TIBETAN PRAYER

The three Buddhist traditions all include prostrations. These are usually performed in front of a statue or image of Buddha, and when Buddhist practitioners enter a temple or shrine room, or greet their teacher, this is usually the first thing they do. If we don't understand the reasons behind the action, this behavior can seem rather odd. People from a Christian background sometimes feel uncomfortable, as at first glance it seems that Buddhists are bowing down to graven images, an act that is prohibited in the Ten Commandments.

We can see that prostrations are actions of devotion and respect but why else do we do them? On one level we are, of course, prostrating to an image of Buddha, but with the attitude of joy and respect that he became enlightened. So it is the qualities he represents that we are paying respect to; we are not mindlessly prostrating to a statue or painting.

Most importantly we are prostrating to our own innate buddhanature, our potential to awaken. By performing the devotional act of prostration with this attitude, we are actively nurturing the Buddha qualities lying latently within us and accumulating merit with the purpose of attaining enlightenment. So prostrations are an act of both humility and respect toward our own Buddha potential.

How to Prostrate

1 We usually prostrate three times in front of the altar when we first enter a shrine room. As we see from the quotation left, we make prostrations not only with our body but also with our speech by silently reciting a prayer praising the three Objects of Refuge – Buddha, Dharma, and Sangha – and with our mind by cultivating respect and faith in the Three Refuges.

2 The three traditions each have their own form of prostrations, which differ slightly. To perform prostrations in the Tibetan way we start in a standing position. We then raise our hands, palms together in salutation above our head, and move our hands in turn to our forehead, our throat and our heart. Then we fall to our hands and knees and touch our forehead to the floor. We stand up and repeat the process till we have done three prostrations in total.

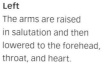

Right
Start the prostration sequence in the standing position.

Left
The arms are raised in salutation and then lowered to the forehead, throat, and heart.

Below
The body is then lowered and the forehead placed on the floor.

Setting up an Altar

Left
Buddhists sometimes pray or meditate at outdoor and indoor shrines. These vary from simple Zen shrines to the wealth of images in Tibetan temples.

> *"If you are so inclined you can set up an altar nearby for pictures that inspire you, for example, or for candles, incense, or other offerings."*
>
> KATHLEEN McDONALD

An altar is not essential for Buddhist meditation but if creating and maintaining an altar appeals to you, then it is an appropriate devotional practice of Buddhism. The different Buddhist traditions have culturally influenced iconography and symbols, which vary in style. A Zen altar is generally very simple, while a Tibetan altar has a whole array of offerings and images. One is not better than the other; they are just following their own tradition.

Below
Anything precious to you or beneficial to your meditation practice – elaborate, traditional, or simple – may be placed on your own altar.

Right
Offerings at a Buddhist shrine in Thailand are a form of people's expression of religious devotion based on what is of value to them in their culture.

We can choose to follow one tradition purely, or draw on several traditions for different meditations or texts. For example, if we decide that we wish to practice only Theravada Buddhism, then it is best to have an altar that reflects this, and our images will be Thai, Burmese, or Sri Lankan in style. If we are just starting and are not quite sure which school of Buddhism suits us best, then we can make a simple altar with any Buddhist images that attract us.

One reason to make an altar with images upon it is to create an atmosphere conducive to our meditation. We can make our altar on a low table or a shelf, on which we can put a statue of one of the Buddhas, or hang a Buddhist picture on the wall. Although we wish to make it beautiful as an offering to the Buddhas, we must remain aware that these paintings and statues have a religious significance; they are not just pretty pictures and ornaments for decoration.

Making Offerings

Another reason to have an altar is to make offerings on a daily basis, or every time we use our room or space for meditation. When we place offerings on our altar, we don't just put physical objects down, we also make inner offerings. This means we are mindful of why we are doing meditation – to awaken to our true nature – so we offer this pure intention to the Buddhas as well.

Traditionally, we offer objects that are pleasing to the senses and have a pure quality. Appropriate offerings are a small bowl of water and a few flowers, also we light a candle and burn some incense. We make the offerings as beautiful as we can since we offer them to Buddha and to our own potential for enlightenment. There is no point in offering inferior objects, or neglecting to change the water daily; such forgetfulness and carelessness would be disrespectful.

CHAPTER FOUR

THERAVADA BUDDHISM

> **❝** *About this mind … in truth there is nothing really wrong with it. It is intrinsically pure. Within itself it is already peaceful. Our practice is simply to see the Original Mind. So we must train the mind to know the sense impressions and not get lost in them. To make it peaceful. Just this is the aim of all this difficult practice we put ourselves through.* **❞**
>
> AJAHN CHAH

Theravada Buddhism

Theravada means "the teachings of the elders," and this tradition can trace its roots to the Sthaviravada school, which developed in India after Buddha's death. In some ways therefore, the forms of Theravada Buddhism are similar to how Buddha and his disciples lived and practiced.

Above
The Yangon Shwedagon Paya Wonder Symbol – Theravada Buddhist temples like this one are common in places like Burma.

Below
Bhikkhus (monks) in the Theravada tradition often live in austere conditions, such as in huts in forests or rural areas.

The language used to chant prayers is Pali, the same language as the bulk of the scriptures, which are known as *suttas* – the collected discourses of Buddha. Together these are called the Pali Canon. Theravada practitioners often pursue either scholarly or meditative inclinations. This is reflected in the two main structures: large temples and monasteries – centers of learning and debate; and the remote, rural meditation monasteries – often simply a few huts in the forest.

In Sri Lanka, Thailand, and Burma, monasticism is considered of prime importance. This appears rather austere at first glance. Monks (known as *bhikkhus*) and nuns eat only one meal a day, which must be taken before noon. This is usually collected on an alms round, in which the monastics walk to where lay supporters live and have food placed in their bowls as an offering. This is considered to earn the donor merit. Sometimes a lay person sponsors a meal at their local monastery.

Monks and nuns are not allowed to handle money or barter for goods, so if their daily meal is not freely given they go without. In practice this rarely happens in the monasteries, but it might occur if a monk is traveling. There are numerous other rules which must also be observed; for example, there are very few possessions a monastic is allowed. Despite the external poverty, and perhaps after an initial period of adjustment, monks and nuns often find a great sense of liberation and joy from this way of life.

Supporting the Monastics

The role of the lay practitioner is largely to support the monastics by donating food regularly. Once a year at the festival called Kathina – which heralds the end of the three months' Rains Retreat – the laity also offer cloth for the monastics' robes. In return they receive spiritual inspiration and advice from the monastics, who also conduct birth, marriage, and death ceremonies.

Theravada Buddhism in the West has developed in different directions to accommodate the different lifestyles and needs of Westerners. However, Theravada monasteries in Europe and America exist, together with Western monks and nuns who uphold this tradition purely and are a great source of spiritual inspiration.

There are also traditional Theravada monasteries in most Western countries, which serve the spiritual needs of Thai, Burmese, and Sri Lankan people living in the West.

Right
Theravada monks (*bhikkhus*) such as these do not handle money and beg for their one meal a day which they eat before noon, going without food if nothing is offered. In return, they offer spiritual inspiration and advice, and conduct birth, marriage, and death ceremonies for lay people.

" *With the ever present, timeless immediacy of 'things as they are' as its central reference point, the Theravada school is a fluid and varied tradition evolving in response to the particular personal, historical, and cultural circumstances of its adherents.* "

GIL FRONSDAL

Above
Shaving heads is usual in the initiation of Theravada monks and nuns, simultaneously removing egotism about their appearance while officially placing them outside ordinary society and social interaction.

> " *… Theravada Buddhism promotes awareness 'techniques' that are simple in themselves, but powerful in their sustained application. It also teaches practices that strengthen such attributes as generosity, lovingkindness, and compassion, thus nurturing the growth of an awakened heart and enabling one to live wisely.* "
>
> GIL FRONSDAL

The majority of Western Theravada practitioners are not monastic but nonetheless practice meditation seriously. They attend meditation and retreat centers regularly, and they are also welcome to visit the monasteries, where anyone who abides by the rules and follows the daily routine can stay for some time. Practitioners usually meditate daily and undertake at least one retreat a year. These range from a few days to three months or longer, but are often around ten to twelve days.

In this way, the Theravada tradition in the West can create space for spiritual practice within the framework of worldly life. Meditation – especially over a period of time in retreat – brings calmness and clarity, which is of great benefit to our usual hectic lives. Yet the purity of the monastic life is also available for those who wish to dedicate their whole lives to Buddhist practice.

The meditation practices of Theravada Buddhism are awareness and mindfulness. In the West this is

Above
This monk in Bangkok, Thailand, receives food alms in his begging bowl. Respect toward monastics remains in many Eastern countries, where people are used to giving food to mendicants.

How Theravada Buddhism Is Practiced

Above
In the East, the feet are considered the lowliest part of the body, so bowing to the Buddha's feet indicates his high status.

generally described as vipassana, or insight meditation, but includes samatha, or calming the mind. Both these practices are based upon the teaching of Buddha found in the Satipatthana Sutta, the Discourse on the Four Foundations of Mindfulness. This begins: "There is, monks, this way that leads only to the purification of beings, to the overcoming of sorrow and distress, to the disappearance of pain and sadness, to the gaining of the right path, to the realization of Nirvana …"

Single-Pointed Attention

Developing our skills in single-pointed attention on an object such as the breath brings quiet concentration. This is not an end in itself, though of course it is pleasant and beneficial to well-being. When the mind is calm we can better observe what is happening inside, and by concentrating upon our thoughts and feelings we develop insight into them. It is this insight that eventually allows us to realize that our delusions, attachment, and aversion are the root of our suffering.

These meditations are supported by the practices of generosity and ethics. By cultivating these qualities we open our hearts to others and realize that they too experience the same suffering as ourselves.

This weakens our self-obsession and helps us realize that we live interdependently with others. So the practical, outer expression of these practices is being of benefit to others, while the inner path gradually leads us to Nibbana, the absence of suffering.

Theravada Buddhism makes the distinction between spiritual and secular activity, which is reflected in the Path of Liberation and the Path of Worldly Well-Being. In practice, these are not separate and reinforce each other. Yet this is a skillful way of realizing that the ultimate aim of our practice is liberation from samsara, the suffering nature of existence, not just living well in this world.

However, enlightenment may take a very long time, so following a way of life which seeks to eliminate suffering is sensible.

A Goenka Retreat

"In the 1970s a spiritual odyssey to India was incomplete without having done an obligatory 'Goenka course.' Goenka started by teaching Indians, but his audience soon came to include the varied Europeans, Americans, and Australians who wandered through the subcontinent in search of religious experience."

STEPHEN BATCHELOR

Above
An Indian meditation teacher from Burma, Satya Narayan Goenka conducts intensive ten-day retreats in India, which became popular with Westerners in the 1970s.

Below left
Burmese temples can be quite elaborate like this one (Schwedagon Pagoda), as there is strong support for Buddhism, the main school of which is Theravada.

Satya Narayan Goenka was born in Burma in 1924, the son of a wealthy Indian family. A meditation retreat by Goenka or one of his teaching disciples lasts ten days. The retreat is conducted in silence, except for talks and instructions by the teacher. Students meditate for ten hours a day, divided into one-hour sessions and short breaks, in a meditation hall, sitting on meditation cushions. Women sit down one side of the hall, men on the other. To those who are unfamiliar with meditation retreats, this can seem a pretty tough regime, so students are encouraged to take a vow of determination to remain for the full ten days.

Initially, students are instructed to observe the sensation of the flow of breath around the nostrils and upper lip. This apparently simple instruction is difficult to maintain, as the mind habitually wanders, distracted by the many thoughts that arise. The teacher will every so often gently remind the students to bring their attention back to the feeling of the breath. There is no sense of punishment as the mind naturally wanders.

Awareness with Equanimity

Gradually the mind becomes more quiet and the attention span lengthens. A sense of peace arises when you are able to focus on the breath for longer stretches of time.

On day four the teacher alters the object of meditation to sensations and now instructs the students to "scan" the body with attention, without moving for the entire session. Starting at the top of the head, students direct their attention to each part of the body in turn. This is to develop choiceless awareness, so we aren't clinging to pleasurable sensations or fighting pain. All sensations are continually changing. By not reacting to different sensations and keeping an open, nonjudgmental mind, we can observe sensations arise and pass. By observing with equanimity when we feel discomfort, we can some- times watch the sensation dissipate without moving. In this way we learn that suffering comes from our reactions to sensations, not from the sensations themselves.

Some sessions will inevitably be agonizing or frustrating, others might be blissful. At the end of the retreat, with silence lifted and benefits shared, many students feel they have survived a difficult internal ordeal and are glad it is over. Yet they also feel they have experienced something very special and many students return to do more retreats, as well as applying the practice in daily life. All retreats are run solely on voluntary donations.

Below
The mind habitually wanders, and the idea is to calm it and focus on the action of the breath. After the mind becomes quiet, the attention span lengthens and a sense of peace arises.

Abhayagiri Monastery

" Abhayagiri means 'Fearless Mountain.' The original Abhayagiri Monastery was in ancient Sri Lanka, at Anuradhapura. That monastery was most notable for welcoming practitioners and teachers from many different Buddhist traditions. "

ABHAYAGIRI MONASTERY
INFORMATION BROCHURE

The community at Abhayagiri Monastery practices the Thai Forest Tradition of Buddhism, as taught by the highly respected teacher Ajahn Chah. The spiritual head is Ajahn Sumedho, head of Amaravati Buddhist Monastery in England, and a senior disciple of Ajahn Chah. Ajahn Amaro and Ajahn Passano are co-abbots of Abhayagiri, the first monastery in America to be founded by Ajahn Chah's disciples.

Abhayagiri was established in 1996 after the generous donation of 120 acres of land in Redwood Valley, California. This was given by Master Hsuan Hua, a Mahayana Buddhist teacher, in an act of spiritual friendship. Ajahn Sumedho and Ajahn Amaro had been visiting and teaching in the area for over a decade, so this opportune gift helped to create a base for the monastic life.

Above Right
Forest-dwelling monks at Abhayagiri Monastery in the US maintain the tradition of the mendicant, carrying begging bowls for alms. The Buddhist concept of interdependence flourishes there.

A Mutually Beneficial Relationship

The Buddhist concept of interdependence flourishes at Abhayagiri in the mutually beneficial relationship between the monastics and their lay supporters. By living a spiritual life of simplicity and purity, the monks and nuns provide an inspiration for lay people to offer support. Thus the monastics survive on the alms provided, and the laity have the opportunity to practice generosity and to use the spiritual sanctuary that the monastery provides. An openness of heart and compassion for each other also develops, which benefits all.

Guests who respect this way of life are welcome to join the daily routine and activities of the community for up to a week, although Abhayagiri Monastery is not a meditation or retreat center. There is no charge but donations toward the upkeep of the monastery are appreciated.

Visitors undertake eight precepts for the duration of their stay. These are:

1. harmlessness
2. trustworthiness
3. celibacy
4. right speech
5. sobriety
6. not eating after noon
7. restraint of the senses by dressing modestly and not seeking entertainment
8. alertness by not sleeping more than necessary

Left
A Mahayana Buddhist master gave 120 acres of land to Ajahn Chah near Lake Tahoe, which is not far from Abhayagiri Monastery in Redwood Valley, California.

Right
This hut in Redwood Valley at Abhayagiri Monastery in the US is the simple kind of dwelling which allows monks to live in the style of bhikkhus.

Left
The Venerable Ajahn Sumedho is an American Buddhist who was taught by Ajahn Chah and is the spiritual head of the Thai forest tradition of Theravada Buddhism in the UK. He oversees monasteries in England, including Chithurst and Amaravati. Monks and nuns work and meditate together, living in separate quarters on the same site.

> "*Ajahn Sumedho ... has proved himself possessed of leadership qualities of an exceptionally high order, with spiritual qualities to match. He also has the ability to put the Dhamma across to Westerners in their own terms, and with humor, lightness, and lucidity.*"
>
> JOHN SNELLING

Ajahn Sumedho was born Robert Jackman in 1934, in America. He started a degree in Far Eastern Studies at the University of Washington, which was interrupted by service as a medical officer in the US Navy during the Korean war. He visited Japan and encountered Buddhism but returned to the States and finished his degree, later taking an MA in Asian Studies.

In 1964 he went with the Peace Corps to Borneo, where he taught English, and afterward visited Thailand. By this time he had started meditating and during a vacation in Laos he was advised to ordain as a monk – which he did at Nong Kai, a temple in northeast Thailand. After a year of solitary practice he joined Ajahn Chah at his monastery, Wat Pah Bong, and remained under his guidance for ten years.

The First Western Abbot in Thailand

Because of Ajahn Chah's reputation, increasing numbers of Westerners began to arrive in Thailand seeking ordination. So in 1974, Wat Pah Nanachat was founded, dedicated to training Western monks.

Above

Chithurst Monastery in England, a mansion with its own surrounding wood, was donated to Sumedho and his followers by a supporter | of Buddhism who was encountered while jogging on Hampstead Heath in London. Today it houses both monks and nuns.

Sumedho subsequently became abbot, the first Westerner to do so in Thailand. However, in 1977, Ajahn Chah was invited to England by the English Sangha Trust, who were trying to establish a community of Western Buddhist monks in England. Ajahn Sumedho accompanied him.

From small beginnings in a house in Hampstead, various monasteries have arisen. These include Chithurst, which has a wood donated by a generous sponsor who was encountered while jogging on Hampstead Heath! Amaravati, just north of London, is the main monastery in England and where Ajahn Sumedho is based. He is the spiritual head of the Thai forest tradition of Buddhism in the UK, and highly respected by both the Thai monastic hierarchy and his Western disciples. Ajahn Sumedho teaches and leads retreats worldwide. Several of his public talks have been recorded and are available.

Left

During break-time and periods of meditation practice at Amaravati Monastery, just north of London, England, monks sit on one side of the room and nuns on the other. Sumedho is based here but teaches and leads retreats all over the world in the Thai Forest Tradition of Theravada Buddhism.

Left
My nursing job does make demands on me but meditation can help me feel at ease.

Below
After going on retreat, I find I have a natural kindness and compassion that I can give to my patients.

I am a nurse at San Francisco General Hospital, which serves the uninsured and poor. I also teach Mindfulness Based Stress Reduction at various hospitals in the San Francisco Bay Area and the San Francisco County Jail. I have been a Buddhist practitioner for 15 years, and for a long time I have been a lay supporter of the Theravada monastics in the Bay Area.

When I leave a retreat, there's a delicious moment of re-entering the busy clinic where I work and feeling completely at ease. There are still endless things to do and a long line of sick patients, but my attitude is different. Instead of the usual irritations and grumbling, I feel a natural kindness I call the "grace period."

Generally I have to work at being kind. My patience is constantly tested by unruly people or a health system that has little to do with health.

After a retreat, I don't have to try to find compassion, it naturally seems to be there. This is the gift I give to my patients.

I remember a ten-day retreat with Ajahn Amaro where I had experienced difficulty staying with thoughts that were raging out of control. I returned to the hospital and met Maria, a young homeless woman who was an addict and had tried repeatedly to commit suicide. Once, she threw herself out of a fifth-story window, and her disfigured face and toothless mouth reflected her injuries from the fall. As she sat in the clinic room she said voices were telling her to harm herself again.

Having recently spent time with my own ruthless mind, I felt I understood what Maria might be experiencing. As we waited for the doctor from Psychiatric Emergency to arrive, we talked. "Tell me Maria, what do you think the voices are?" "I think they are my own thoughts," she replied. I found myself telling her my own experience of my thoughts dwelling on a violence that had happened long ago, a violence that still felt lodged somewhere in my body. Maria nodded.

Connecting with Maria

From that moment, Maria and I were connected, and a bond grew between us. She sought me out for advice and assistance concerning her numerous challenges. I collected art supplies for her so that she could paint pictures to calm herself down and express her wandering thoughts. Once, she gave me a pink candle as a present. "When you light it, think of me," she said. Eventually Maria was able to find a place to live where she was more comfortable with herself, though she still exists very close to a nightmarish edge.

Above

When I spend time with my own ruthless and questioning mind, I am able to understand more clearly the patients who have problems within their own minds. I find that we aren't so different.

Often we see people through the veil of our images and stereotypes. In hospitals, people are labeled with diagnoses. According to conventional psychiatric wisdom, there is a huge difference between a psychotic and a "normal" person. My experience in meditation has shown me that my mind is not so different from Maria's. The voices she heard were another manifestation of what I had encountered in my own mind. I told Maria, "You have a choice. You don't have to believe your thoughts." I knew I was telling her what I needed to hear.

According to Buddha, we are all crazy as we operate within the realm of greed, hatred, and delusion. The cure the Buddha offers is tasting the truth by stopping and sitting in meditation. It's difficult to express how much sitting meditation means to me. It feels like it has saved my life.

THE MONKS AND THE OLD WOMAN

Once upon a time two Theravada bhikkhus, or monks, were traveling together, making the long journey between two monasteries. The way was arduous over hills, through forests, and over streams and rivers. One day they came to a wide river swollen by rainwater and rushing over rocks. It was just possible for the two bhikkhus to wade across as they were strong, healthy young men. They decided to wander down the river bank to look for the best place to attempt their crossing.

As they walked by the side of the river they encountered an old woman sitting by a suitable place to cross. She had obviously been waiting a long time and was pleased to see people who might be able to offer assistance. She politely requested the bhikkhus to help her, and told them she had been waiting for two days for someone to come and was now desperate to get to the other side.

One bhikkhu declined to help her, turned away, and started wading into the water. The other bhikkhu picked her up and put her on his back, then walked slowly and carefully across the river. When he reached the far bank he gently put her down and walked on quickly to rejoin his companion who had strode on ahead.

They walked in silence for a while but there was a tension in the air, making an uncomfortable atmosphere. Finally the bhikkhu who had not assisted the woman turned angrily to his companion. "You should not have carried the old woman across the river! You know it breaks the precepts for a monk to touch a woman!"

The bhikkhu who had helped the old woman across the river looked sadly at his fellow monk and replied, "Ah, but I put her down when we had finished crossing the river. You, my friend, are still carrying her."

What We Can Learn from This Story

So what can we learn from this story? The unhelpful bhikkhu was correct in his understanding of the Theravada precept; a monk should not touch a woman. However, Buddhism is more than a rigid set of rules and allows for personal interpretation of different circumstances.

The bhikkhu who carried the old woman across the river acted spontaneously out of compassion for her plight, and this took precedence over an inflexible adherence to the rules. The other bhikkhu who followed the rule blindly without question allowed this to prevent him helping someone in need.

Furthermore, he became angry and self-righteous and instead of letting the event pass when it was over, continued feeling these negative emotions. The helpful bhikkhu was being skillful in pointing this out when he answered that the first bhikkhu was still carrying the old woman. He had seen that in these particular circumstances an act of compassionate assistance was more important than blindly adhering to the precept, and simply accepted it, letting it pass once the event was over.

We could say therefore that the moral of the story is that the precepts are there to guide, help, instruct, and strengthen those who follow them. They are not absolutes to replace a sense of personal responsibility.

Below

Even though the Theravada bhikkhu was not meant to touch the old woman, carrying her across the river showed that Theravada precepts can be flexible in extreme circumstances.

Going for Refuge

Above
Initiation into Buddhist traditions is called "taking refuge." This woman is formalizing her desire to learn from this particular teacher whom she respects as someone who can lead her to enlightenment.

> "Going for Refuge gives a continual perspective on life by referring one's conduct and understanding to the qualities of Buddha (wisdom), *Dhamma* (truth), *and Sangha* (virtue)."
>
> AJAHN SUMEDHO

Below
Certain formalities between teachers and students of Buddhism are generally observed. However, set guidelines govern essential practices in every Buddhist tradition.

Requesting the Three Refuges

The formal way for a lay person to request the Three Refuges from a Theravada bhikkhu or nun is as follows. (The words are traditionally chanted or spoken in Pali, so this is given first. For a man, the first of the two words separated by / is used, for a woman the second.)

1   Bow from the waist three times, holding the hands in the anjali posture, as shown.

2   Chant or speak the following recitation, being mindful of the meaning:

MAYAM/AHAM BHANTE (AYYE) TI-SARANENA SAHA PANCA SILANI YACAMA/YACAMI
I, Venerable Sir (or Sister), request the Three Refuges.

DUTTYAMPI MAYAM/AHAM BHANTE (AYYE) TI-SARANENA SAHA PANCA SILANI YACAMA/YACAMI
For the second time, Venerable Sir, I request the Three Refuges.

TATIYAMPI MAYAM/AHAM BHANTE (AYYE) TI-SARANENA SAHA PANCA SILANIA YACAMA/YACAMI
For the third time, Venerable Sir, I request the Three Refuges.

3   The bhikkhu or nun recites the following words three times;
The lay person then recites them three times:

NAMO TASSA BHAGAVATO ARAHATO SAMMASAMBUDDHASSA
Homage to the Blessed One, the Noble One, and Perfectly Enlightened One.

4   The bhikkhu or nun recites the following line by line,
which the lay person repeats line by line:

BUDDHAM SARANAM GACCHAMI
To the Buddha I go for Refuge.

DHAMMAM SARANAM GACCHAMI
To the Dhamma I go for Refuge.

SANGHAM SARANAM GACCHAMI
To the Sangha I go for Refuge.

5   These three lines are repeated three times:
(prefix DUTTYAMPI/ for the second time, and
TATTYAMPI/ for the third time)

6   The bhikkhu or nun says:
TISARANA – GAMANAM NITTHITAM
This completes the going to the Three Refuges.

7   The lay person responds:
AMA BHANTE (AYYE)
Yes, Venerable Sir (or Sister)

Right
To request the Three Refuges as a lay person, the hands must be held in the anjali posture.

Meditation on Lovingkindness

"*Metta is a Pali word meaning 'lovingkindness' or 'friendship.' It is part of the living tradition of Buddhist meditation practices that cultivates spaciousness of mind and openness of heart.*"

SHARON SALZBERG

Above
A Buddhist monk in Thailand blesses a car for someone's safety. Blessings of this kind are sometimes given by Buddhist monks.

Below
The practice of cultivating loving feelings is called *metta* in Buddhism – described as general "lovingkindness" toward all sentient beings.

With metta meditation we work with phrases. These are not spoken aloud, just mentally repeated, but we try to allow the phrases to emerge naturally from our heart. We cultivate our feelings, not our intellect.

Meditation on Lovingkindness

1 Sit comfortably and relax. Develop the motivation to have enough attention for the mind not to wander but not so much that it becomes obsessive.

2 We first develop lovingkindness toward ourselves. Sometimes we feel we don't deserve to be happy or we judge ourselves harshly. Loving and accepting ourselves is the first step toward developing lovingkindness for others.

3 Silently say: "May I live in safety. May I experience mental happiness, peace, and joy. May I have physical happiness, health, and no pain. May my daily life go easily, without difficulty." These are traditional phrases, but if we like we can make up our own that are personally meaningful.

4 After about five minutes, bring to mind someone who has helped you, like a Buddhist teacher or similar benefactor. Repeat the phrases using their name and feel lovingkindness for them.

5 After five minutes include a good friend, then a person toward whom you feel neutral. This latter might be difficult, so remind yourself that this person for whom you have no strong feelings wishes to be free from suffering and to be happy, just like yourself.

6 Finally include an enemy, a person who has harmed you or toward whom you have negative feelings. Reflect that you don't have to like the person or condone their negative behavior, but you can develop lovingkindness toward them by not wishing them harm. Often people who behave badly experience much suffering, so offering them lovingkindness can be helpful.

7 Finish by including all beings and reflecting on how you are interdependent with everyone. Dedicate any merit generated from your meditation to the happiness of all beings.

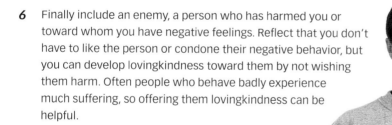

Right
The first step toward lovingkindness is to feel it for ourselves – this might be more difficult than you think.

The Mantra "Buddho"

"*If you've got a really active thinking mind, you may find the mantra 'Buddho' helpful. . . . The word 'Buddho' is a word you can develop in your life as something to fill the mind with rather than with worries. . . . It means 'the one who knows,' the Buddha, 'the awakened,' 'that which is awake.'*"

AJAHN SUMEDHO

Left
The Medicine Buddha expounded all of the Tibetan medical tantras, the cures for all human afflictions, such as an overactive mind.

The Mantra "Buddho"

Work with the mantra "Buddho" silently, repeating the word in your mind, as you did with the lovingkindness phrases. This meditation helps with concentration and can be practiced on its own or interspersed with other meditations.

1 Start by observing the sensation of the breath entering and leaving your nostrils.

2 Then for each inhalation silently repeat, or bring to mind, the syllable "Bud."

3 For each exhalation use "dho." We keep our attention on the sensation of breathing as well as on "Bud" and "dho."

4 Try to bring your attention to each syllable, each time. Keep it bright, clear, and alive; don't just slip into repeating the sound passively and mindlessly.

5 When thoughts interrupt "Buddho," remember that for the next 10 or 15 minutes the occasion has arisen to do only this. Be fully present with "Buddho," you can think your thoughts freely afterward.

6 Don't use "Buddho" to suppress thoughts. By patiently and gently imposing "Buddho" on your thoughts, they gradually and naturally fade out.

7 If you become bored and think, "This is silly," or "I don't want to do this," simply observe the thought and let it go. Don't be critical or judge yourself harshly; it is natural for these thoughts to arise but you don't have to indulge them.

8 Try to let go of ideas of success or failure, these are the greatest obstacle to concentration. Instead of thinking "I'm doing this well" or "I can't do this," learn to see where your mind tends to wander and note the habitual patterns.

9 Don't avoid unpleasant thoughts and indulge nice ones; they are all simply just thoughts.

Right
Meditating with a mantra can help the focus on each inhalation and exhalation.

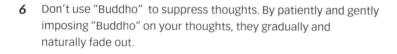

Mindfulness of the Ordinary

Above
A Buddhist monk practices walking meditation in Sri Lanka, the idea being to note how we do things which we usually do without thinking in ordinary life.

Below
Noting bodily sensations as they arise and pass is part of being mindful while one practices both sitting and walking meditation.

"We use the ordinary breath, not a special breathing practice; the sitting posture rather than standing on our heads; normal walking rather than running, jogging, or walking methodically slowly – just a relaxed pace. We're practicing around what's most ordinary, because we take it for granted. But now we're bringing our attention to all the things we've taken for granted and never noticed, such as our minds and bodies."

AJAHN SUMEDHO

Mindfulness of the Ordinary

We can do this meditation alternating between walking and sitting for 10 to 15 minutes each. This meditation reminds us that we are usually distracted by what is extraordinary: exciting events that happen to us or just watching television – even programs about "normal" life include lots of drama in order to hold our attention.

1 Start walking mindfully along your walking path, no faster or slower than usual. When you reach the end, pause, then turn and walk to the other end.

2 Become aware of each foot stepping on to the path, lifting off and moving forward.

3 Reflect how you normally take walking for granted, because it is an ordinary activity we do all the time. Be really mindful of each step.

4 Notice your other bodily sensations as they arise and pass. Then try to notice what the different parts of your body feel like when there is no particular sensation.

5 After 10 or 15 minutes, move into the sitting posture. Be mindful of how you usually take this movement for granted and be fully present as you change your position.

6 Begin to focus on the sensation of the breath entering and leaving your body. Start with the nostrils, then bring your attention to the rise and fall of your diaphragm.

7 Be careful not to change your breathing pattern. The practice is observation of the breath; there is no good or bad way of breathing.

8 Reflect how your body breathes even when you are unaware of it.

9 Try to be with your breathing without making it special.

10 You can, however, reflect on the preciousness and fragility of your existence.

11 At the end of your meditation resolve to continue being mindful of your mind and body as you move into other activities.

소원 성취

丁ㅇ鎮
丁겨운

'95.8.15
父母 기원

소 원 성 취
김
진행이윤차안정
국 군 군 군 군 철훈

김선연

어령군 옹ㅇ면 소ㅇ리

동양기와
전화85-6087-2336

소원성취
소원
백성연
서울 잠실

소원성
백주호
성연

CHAPTER FIVE

ZEN BUDDHISM

 *In Zen, everything one does becomes a vehicle for self-realization; every act, every movement is done wholeheartedly, with nothing left over. . . . For what else is there but the pure act? . . . Everything else – thoughts of the past, fantasies about the future . . . what are these but shadows and ghosts flickering about in our minds, preventing us from entering fully into life itself? To enter into the awareness of Zen, to 'wake up' means to cleanse the mind of the habitual disease of uncontrolled thought and to bring it back to its original state of purity and clarity.* **99**

PHILIP KAPLEAU

Zen originated when the Indian monk Bodhidharma went to China in the sixth century and challenged the existing Buddhist status quo, which he found overly scholastic. His approach was simple directness – to wake up to our true nature in the here and now. Zen therefore emphasizes meditation rather than study, though Buddhist principles underlie the practices.

Below
A Zen master strikes monks who request it during meditation practice with a wooden stick. Zen practitioners aim to stay alert at all times so that their practice remains dynamic and they awaken fully to their own "buddhanature."

The purpose of Zen is to see directly into your own self-nature; all other endeavors and aims are purposeless – even striving for enlightenment. This stark approach allows for the possibility of awakening in the present moment, rather than gradually becoming enlightened through accumulating merit and clocking up many hours of meditation.

Zen masters are sometimes renowned for their bizarre behavior, which can appear rather un-Buddhist. This includes shouting at and striking disciples, which is designed to startle a disciple out of his or her usual thought patterns and behavior. These are therefore actually skillful actions arising from the master's compassion to help the disciple awaken in the here and now.

This story about Alan Watts is an example of the bizarre behavior of some Zen teachers. Already successful in America, Watts was invited to lecture in England in 1953. He strode dramatically onto the stage at Caxton Hall, stood still for a moment, then

"The way of the Buddha is to know yourself, to know yourself is to forget yourself, to forget yourself is to be enlightened by all things."

DOGEN

Above

Japanese Zen Buddhism approves of the student who has a questioning mind, for Zen masters say that only great doubt enables | great awakening. Without doubt, one risks complacency, which does not contribute to the goal of presence of mind or alertness.

The Three Attitudes

Great Faith is believing in our own buddhanature, not in anything outside of ourselves. This is reflected in a popular but often misunderstood Zen saying: "If you see the Buddha walking down the road, kill him!" This does not refer to Shakyamuni Buddha but to when we lose faith in our potential buddhahood and project it on to someone else. Of course we have respect for our Zen master and might believe him or her to be enlightened, but not at the expense of our own potential.

We need Great Courage to follow the Zen path. There are many stories of extreme measures undertaken by practitioners to help them stay alert. The Korean master Kusan Sunim would sit at the edge of a cliff to meditate; the fear of falling off kept his meditation dynamic. In some Japanese meditation halls (known as *zendos*), the windows are opened in winter and shut in summer. This helps develop the Great Courage needed to stay meditating in challenging conditions. We also need Great Courage to keep meditating even when we don't think we are getting anywhere, to let go of our fantasies, and to calm our wandering mind.

Great Questioning is also known as Great Doubt. We might wonder why doubt is part of the Zen path but it is the inspiration to keep questioning that is meant, not distrust or apprehension. The well-known Zen saying: "Great Doubt, Great Awakening; Little Doubt, Little Awakening; No Doubt, No Awakening," clearly expresses the concept that questioning is integral to awakening.

shouted, "Wake up!" The stunned audience made no response. Watts tried again but to no avail, so he launched into a conventional lecture on how we are all asleep!

Zen practitioners undertake the three trainings of ethics, meditation, and wisdom, which are based on general Buddhist principles. They are also encouraged to cultivate the Three Attitudes of:

1. Great Faith
2. Great Courage
3. Great Questioning

Right

Everything in a Zen monastery is set up in order to encourage simplicity and order, so that practitioners' external surroundings reflect the inner workings of an orderly mind. Meals are no exception, as this simple and orderly lunch at a Zen monastery shows.

How Zen Buddhism Is Practiced

The original Chinese Zen Buddhism, Ch'an, gradually declined but it did pass to Korea and Japan, where Zen flourished and developed. It also passed to Vietnam, where it combined with Pure Land Buddhism. Two distinct traditions survived in Japan, and contemporary Zen is based on these. Both traditions share some features and are not as clearly demarcated in practice today as they once were. Traditionally, the form was monasticism, though lay people, including women, could receive training if they wished. The main feature of Zen practice is sitting meditation – known as *zazen* – with the aim of awakening to your true nature.

Soto Zen, founded by Dogen, has as its main practice intensive sitting meditation, called *Shikantaza*. The idea that we are actually buddhas when we sit in meditation – not just potential buddhas who have not yet awakened – is central to the Soto tradition. Meditators traditionally sit facing the wall. Rinzai Zen, founded by Eisai, also has a practice of

Above
Practical activities like building and gardening form part of life at a Zen monastery, as at all other Buddhist monasteries. Additional activities may include flower arranging or tea making.

sitting meditation; but koan practice is the distinctive feature. Korean Zen, known as Son, also incorporates koans, called *hwadus* in Korea.

Koans (Hwadus)

A koan or hwadu is a paradoxical question or

Right
Korean nuns traditionally meditate together in the temple. Traditional religious practitioners can offer guidance and advice, as they are accomplished meditators themselves.

Below Left
This Zen monk practicing *zazen* or sitting meditation in a Kyoto sand garden in Japan is wide awake, having been trained by Zen masters intent on startling students into being alert at all times.

phrase. Some koans have become familiar in the West, such as, "What is the sound of one hand clapping?" However, this has led to the misconception that a koan is a riddle that can be solved.

The real function of a koan is to break our habitual ways of thinking and thereby awaken and so should not be approached with the idea that there is an answer. By continuously questioning, we try to bypass our usual conceptual and intellectual mind, and "be the koan."

Regular meditation practice is desirable – particularly periods of intensive retreat, called *sesshin*. This takes place in the zendo with a group of students. The traditional importance of the Zen master continues today. Meditators have regular interviews and an intense – but usually impersonal – relationship often develops. This focus on the students' meditation practice rather than their ego identity facilitates the teacher to monitor the students' progress. In this way the Zen master can help with any obstacles and assist their disciples' development.

> " *Zen is a special transmission outside of scriptures; it doesn't rely on words or letters. It is a direct pointing to the human heart and the realization of buddhahood.* "
>
> BODHIDHARMA

A Korean Zen Retreat

Left
Martine and Stephen Batchelor learned in Korea the kind of Buddhism that they teach in Britain. They call it "radical questioning" and offer silent week-long retreats once a year at Gaia House in Devon. Sitting, walking, and questioning practices are all undertaken.

> " *Stephen Batchelor and his wife Martine run what they call 'Radical Questioning' retreats in Britain, based on the Korean Zen training that they received under Kusan Sunim (1908– 1983) at Songgwang Sa, a monastery in Cholla Namdo province, south- west Korea.* "
>
> JOHN SNELLING

Korean monastic meditation is based on three-month retreat periods interspersed with three-month free periods. During retreats, practitioners meditate for ten to fourteen hours a day. This is obviously not practical for lay Western students so it has been adapted, but sensitively, to keep the original flavor.

Retreats last a week and are currently held once a year at Gaia House in Devon. Silence is maintained for the full week, except for an interview. The daily schedule starts at 6:15 am with the first sitting. Each sitting, except the first and last, is followed by brisk walking round the meditation hall for ten minutes. Sittings last thirty-five minutes and the total practice time each day is eight and a half hours, though students can do more if they wish.

Before the first and the last session traditional prostrations are done, accompanied by water and incense offerings. A traditional wooden stick (called a *jukpi*), held by a teacher, is slapped into the hand, marking the start and end of sessions. Morning instruction and evening talks are also given to the students.

For the first couple of days, students are instructed in breath meditation to quiet the mind.

Left
After the retreat has ended participants discuss their experiences so that they can compare theirs with those of others.

Below
This Korean statue symbolizes the awakened state of a Buddha.

Then the hwadu, "What is this?" is introduced. Students are instructed to repeat the question silently but to have no expectation of an answer. When the mind wanders, it is gently brought back to the question. If the mind becomes dull, students are advised to intensify the questioning, if overexcited, returning to the breath is suggested.

The questioning is not cerebral and students are taught to question from the area just below the navel, which is an energy center called the tanden. Though this might sound odd, in practice it keeps the energy grounded in the body and helps prevent the onset of headaches.

The Spaciousness of Not Knowing

After some time, students are instructed to rest for a while in the unknowing space that arises naturally from questioning without expecting an answer. When the mind wanders, the student returns to the question. The spaciousness of not knowing helps free the mind from clinging to our usual self-identification, and interdependence with the people and environment around can be experienced.

During the interview, the teacher and student discuss the student's practice and questions can be answered. The retreat formally ends on the last morning and students are encouraged to talk with each other. A final group "go-round" allows each person to see their individual experience in relation to others. This retreat is suitable for people who already have experience of meditation.

The Rochester Zen Center

> *"The [Rochester Zen] Center is one of the longest-established Buddhist communities in the United States, and offers authentic Zen training in a Western context."*
>
> ROCHESTER ZEN CENTER INFORMATION LEAFLET

The Rochester Zen Center was founded by Roshi Philip Kapleau in 1966. He began a spiritual quest after his experience as chief court reporter at the Nuremberg Trials, held at the end of the Second World War. Listening day after day to the appalling testimonies of the witnesses caused a dilemma that only a deep spiritual understanding could resolve.

In 1953, he arrived at a Zen Buddhist monastery in Japan and began a training that lasted thirteen years, studying first with Harada-Roshi and then his successor, Yasutami-Roshi, known as his Dharma heir. On his return to America he set up the Rochester Zen Center and published *The Three Pillars of Zen*, a classic book for Western Zen students.

Roshi Kapleau has now retired from teaching but remains a great inspiration to those at the Center. The Spiritual Director is currently Sensei Bodhin Kjolhede, Roshi Kapleau's Dharma heir. The Rochester Zen Center follows a tradition of integral Zen, combining elements from both Rinzai and Soto schools – the two major traditions in Japan. Rochester is one of the foremost training centers for Zen students in America.

A Full-Time Zen Training

The Rochester Zen Center is specifically designed to
accommodate students engaged in full-time
training in Zen Buddhism. The Center does not cater
to casual visitors and does not encourage people to
visit in this way. There are other Zen centers that
provide facilities for those making initial inquiries
into Zen Buddhism. However, for those interested in
joining the training, there is a one-day workshop,
held every other month on a Saturday. This provides
a comprehensive introduction to Zen and is the first
step to becoming a member of the Center.

Students follow a daily schedule starting with
morning zazen at 5:45 am. During the workday
there is a period of zazen after morning tea and a
formal lunch at 12:30 pm. The workday ends with
chanting at 3:30 pm. On Sundays there is a Dharma
talk (called a *teisho*), after the morning zazen, and the
rest of the day is free. Approximately every other
month there is a seven-day sesshin (retreat), and
there are other shorter sesshins throughout the year.
Members can have three private interviews, called
dokusan, each week with the teacher.

Various Buddhist ceremonies are also observed,
including commemorating Vesak (Buddha's
birthday) and Bodhidharma Day (which honors the
founder of the Zen tradition). A ceremony called
Jukai (the taking of the precepts) is held in
November. Thanksgiving and New Year are also
celebrated at the Rochester Zen Center.

Above
Full-time Zen training is available
at the Rochester Zen Center in
Rochester, New York, where only
serious practitioners are encouraged to come for periodic retreats
of seven days.

Thich Nhat Hanh

"*Thich Nhat Hanh is now widely regarded as one of the leading teachers and interpreters of Buddhism in the West.*"

STEPHEN BATCHELOR

Left
This Vietnamese Zen Buddhist monk became a leader in the non-violent protest movement against the war in South Vietnam in the 1960s. Now banned from returning home, he resides in France.

Below
The number of Thich Nhat Hanh's followers in the West is rising every year, partly as a result of his book, entitled *Being Peace,* which has sold over 150,000 copies. He is also active as a peace movement spokesman.

Thich Nhat Hanh was born Nguyen Xuan Bao in Vietnam in 1926. He received a normal education, including exposure to Western ideas. At age sixteen he entered Tu Hieu Zen Monastery and started a monastic Zen training. This continued peacefully until his life was dramatically changed by the conflict in Vietnam between the Communist North and anti-Communist South, and the resulting war with America.

The Buddhists began to be persecuted by the Catholic dictatorship in South Vietnam, so the recently formed All Vietnamese Buddhist Association started to promote Buddhism as a unifying force in their divided country. Thich Nhat Hanh became the editor of their magazine and his skilled commitment to nonviolent protest and Buddhism led to an invitation in 1961 to teach Buddhism at Columbia University, America.

Thich Nhat Hanh returned in 1964 and helped found the Van Hanh University in Saigon. The following year he published a volume of poetry wishing for peace and criticizing the war. As a result he was denounced by both sides and an assassination attempt was made – which narrowly failed. Undeterred, he founded the Tiep Hien Order, which means Order of Interbeing, promoting a Buddhism that emphasized social responsibility and pacifism with a foundation of mindful awareness.

Above
There are Western nuns under Hanh's guidance who follow the traditional ways of Buddhist nuns. Particular emphasis is placed upon remaining conscious of the present moment while continuing to take part in the world that exists around.

Plum Village

Thich Nhat Hanh then toured Europe and America, giving talks on Buddhism and trying to bring attention to the suffering in Vietnam. After the signing of the Peace Accords in Paris in 1973, he was banned from returning to Vietnam and accordingly settled in rural France. There he founded Plum Village, a Buddhist community for Vietnamese refugees, and continued as a spokesman for the Vietnamese Buddhist peace movement. There are increasing numbers of visitors there, and Buddhist retreats are held each summer.

Thich Nhat Hanh was nominated for the Nobel Peace Prize in 1967 by Martin Luther King, Jr. His books offer simple but profound Buddhist teachings and poetry, emphasizing engaged Buddhism. His book *Being Peace* has sold over 150,000 copies and has been translated into nine languages.

Below
Retreats are held every summer by Thich Nhat Hanh at Plum Village in France, where he has founded a Buddhist community for Vietnamese refugees. His teaching emphasizes strict moral precepts.

Zen Personal View – Amy Hollowell

My path begins right here. Out the window and through the bushes in wild bloom, I have an ageless view of the back garden wall, its crumbling gray stone topped by burnt-red tiles, awash in the hesitant sunlight of midafternoon during the spring.

My path begins right now. The telephone's unexpected ring startles me before I answer, taking a call for someone else. A wicked late-season cold has me weary and raw-nosed, finding respite in strong hot tea. With each sip I am right here, now, where my path always begins and where it never ends. Here it just goes ever deeper into the unfathomable reaches of each and every perfect moment.

This path is my life. Sitting in meditation affords me a panoramic view of this path, which is simply all things just as they are, endlessly. When I consider what might make mine a so-called Zen life, I find nothing that can be called Zen and not be called my life, and nothing that can be called my life and not be called Zen.

To practice Zen is to practice my life. This is to live it truly and completely, no holds barred, to soar flat out, spread-eagle into the sublime cross-fire of right now. It is to live it all. Or better, it is to be it all – to be completely who and what I am, whoever and whatever that might be. A wise Chinese poet wrote that this, the perfect way, is easy; it just dislikes picking and choosing.

But of course we pick and choose who we want and do not want to be all the time and so fail to see who we really are. When my second child was an infant, my body didn't produce enough breast milk to nourish him, so at each feeding he needed a supplemental bottle. I was devastated. What a terrible, inadequate mother I was! I was nothing like what I thought I should be, which caused me great suffering at a time when I was already exhausted and overwhelmed by the demands of caring for two small children.

Left
Life in rural France can be idyllic for a Zen practitioner who appreciates every moment of life, and knows that at any time one may experience life completely without restriction or limitation. The only limitation is that which we bring to it. Perceived correctly, we see that "infinite abundance" is at the heart of everything we observe and encounter.

This not looking elsewhere is my path. I can practice while sitting in meditation or folding laundry. The truth is everywhere, but to see it I have to be there. I used to hate rain because humidity makes my hair frizzy, and I wanted my hair to be straight. When it rained, I had frizzy hair and became insufferable.

Once I let go of having my hair a certain way, I could let go of having the world a certain way and be drenched in its rich downpour. Everything and everyone are at every moment like raindrops, marvels of pure goodness. At the heart of each instant there is nothing but this, in infinite abundance.

Wherever I look I see it. You are this, splendidly. And this, right here, is my perfect way.

Doing What Had to be Done

Finally, I could do only what needed to be done. I fed and bathed the children, held, comforted, and loved them. Months passed. They grew. They thrived. And so, when I had dropped the ideas about what sort of mother I should be, did I. I had caught myself looking elsewhere for what had been right here all along: the perfect mother of two perfect children.

BODHIDHARMA

Bodhidharma is a legendary Zen figure, and is credited with being the First Patriarch – great teacher – of Chinese Ch'an, or Zen, arriving in China in the sixth century from South India. The following story shows how his severe approach was ultimately of benefit to his students, helping them to attain enlightenment.

Bodhidharma had been meditating for nine years in the Shaolin Temple, facing the wall according to the traditional way of Ch'an meditation. A monk arrived and requested teaching, but Bodhidharma refused. Desperate to gain the master's attention the monk eventually took a sword in his right hand and chopped off his left arm as a sign of his sincerity.

This dramatic act caught Bodhidharma's attention, and he at once agreed to talk with the monk, who made an earnest request. "My soul is not at peace. Please, master, pacify it for me." "Bring your soul here and I'll pacify it," replied Bodhidharma. After a pause the monk admitted, "I've been looking for it for ages, but have found no trace of it." "There you are!" the master exclaimed, "It's pacified once and for all."

Bodhidharma was not being cruel to the monk; his reticence allowed the monk to ponder his question deeply, and strengthen his determination to awaken. Cutting off his arm was a sign of nonattachment to his body, and demonstrated his commitment to the spiritual path.

However, this story does not mean we should go around mutilating ourselves to impress our teachers! As with many other Zen stories, we can regard this as a metaphor rather than an actual account. What is important is not whether the story is factually true, but whether we see the truth in it.

Left
When the monk cut off his left arm this act showed his great commitment to the spiritual path and was a sign of his nonattachment to his body.

What Is This?

The next story is not pure Zen, more of a cross-cultural encounter between two Buddhist traditions, but it has a Zen flavor. It is a contemporary tale, told to me by a friend who was an assistant to one of the teachers.

A renowned Zen master and a renowned Tibetan lama were to have a meeting. The encounter was eagerly anticipated by the students who would accompany their teachers, and they expected to hear wonderful discourses on the Dharma. Neither teacher had had previous exposure to the other teacher's tradition.

The great day finally arrived. The Tibetan lama walked into the room where the Zen master was waiting. Dispensing with formalities in true Zen style, the Zen master seized an orange from a fruit bowl on the table and flourished it at the Tibetan lama. "What is this?" he demanded, a traditional Zen koan.

The Tibetan lama appeared a little startled by this behavior. He turned to one of his assistants and said, "What's the matter? Hasn't he ever seen an orange before?"

This is very funny, but there is a valuable lesson, too. Neither teacher was immediately able to understand the other's approach, because they came from different cultures, and therefore had different interpretations of the Dharma. This does not mean they were lesser teachers, merely that Dharma is culturally conditioned to some extent.

We can think of this story if we meet a Japanese, Korean, or any other Asian Buddhist teacher and do not understand what they are saying or doing. Even though the Dharma ultimately is universal, we might need in the first instance to understand something of our teacher's culture, too.

Left
The story of the monks and the orange show how different cultures have different interpretations of the Dharma. Even though the Dharma is universal, an understanding of culture is important too.

Zen and the Arts

> *"Every human action may be undertaken as an exercise toward Enlightenment and performed in such a way as to suggest the ineffable. Thus Zen Buddhism has given the world Zen archery, Zen karate, Zen swordsmanship, Zen flower-arranging, Zen tea-drinking, and the art of Zen dance."*
>
> SUN OCK LEE

Zen Buddhism could be said to regard life as an art, where every moment can be lived in complete mindfulness in order to awaken. So many ritual art forms arose naturally as part of Zen practice. For example, the Zen master Thich Nhat Hanh writes poems known as *gathas*, which help people perform daily tasks mindfully.

Some forms of Zen art – like tea ceremonies – emphasize ritual as a technique to remain mindful and in the moment. Each implement is placed in an exact position and used precisely; each movement of taking the cup and drinking is performed in a particular way. The unswerving formality and ritual are combined with exquisite delicacy and grace, so the whole ceremony becomes an offering of mindfulness.

Left
Every human action may be undertaken as enlightened activity or used as a method toward attaining enlightenment. Even flower-arranging is a sacred art form. The care given to any activity will show in the result.

Zen Calligraphy

Other forms of Zen art, like calligraphy, combine mindfulness with spontaneity. The Zen master (in some cases an ordinary lay person) sits in mindful meditation in front of paper, brush, and ink. Suddenly, with one swift movement he or she paints a syllable. Syllables have a symbolic meaning, like the Chinese character *Mu* meaning "no," which is a koan. The master discards all that are confused (though to the untrained eye this is often indiscernible) and repeats the whole exercise until harmony is attained.

Finally, in the following poem we see how Zen archery makes the act itself a mindfulness practice; aiming for anything is simply a distraction.

Below
Concentration upon the action enables one to be both mindful and spontaneous. Zen archers are aware of this, or its loss, each time they shoot an arrow.

Right
Zen calligraphers when writing also perfect a meditative state, where every stroke must be carefully considered and undertaken so that no errors are made.

NEED TO WIN

When an archer is shooting for nothing
he has all his skill.

If he shoots for a brass buckle he is
already nervous.
If he shoots for a prize of gold
he goes blind
or sees two targets –
he is out of his mind!

His skill has not changed
But the prize divides him. He cares.

He thinks more of winning than of shooting.
And the need to win drains him of power.

Chuang Tzu

Zen Breathing Meditation

Above
Amida Buddha, the Buddha of limitless light, is one of the main practices of Pure Land Buddhism. Practitioners repeat Amida's mantra as much as possible.

Below
Japanese statue of the bodhisattva Kannon, who is known as Avalokiteshvara in Indian Mahayana Buddhism.

" *In truth I say to you that within this fathom-high body, with its thoughts and perceptions, lies the world and the rising of the world and the ceasing of the world, and the Way that leads to the extinction of rising and ceasing.* "

SHAKYAMUNI BUDDHA

Zen Breathing Meditation

This is a good meditation to focus the mind and calm the thoughts. It can be practiced by itself, or as a preparation for either zazen or koan meditation. In all Zen meditations posture is considered very important, so before starting, remind yourself of one of the correct ways to sit that is comfortable for you.

1 Sit in the correct posture. Settle comfortably and resolve not to move unless absolutely necessary for the duration of the meditation.

2 Take two or three deep breaths and then allow the breathing to find its natural rhythm and pace.

3 Start counting your breaths; each inhalation and exhalation count as one.

4 Remain mindful of the whole breath, not just at the end when you count.

5 When your mind wanders, start again at the beginning and count one for the next full breath.

6 Traditionally, we aim to count up to ten and start again. However, in practice we rarely go beyond five without the mind wandering. Be careful not to cheat; there is simply no purpose as this is a method to calm the mind, not a competition.

7 Frustration often arises. This seems to be a very simple meditation but in practice it is very difficult. If you feel frustrated just regard it as another thought; let it go without trying to suppress it, and start counting at the beginning again.

8 Our minds tend to be excitable at the beginning but have faith that the thoughts will slow down eventually, and let go of depression if it arises. This is simply the nature of the mind in meditation.

9 If you manage to reach ten, check whether you are really being mindful for the whole time. Then start at one again.

Right
Posture is very important when you are undertaking a Zen meditation.

Zazen Meditation

Above
These monks are possibly simply reminding themselves through their practice that there is nothing to attain, but only the need to "wake up" to experience their true buddhanature.

Below
Buddhist ceremonial practice is not only confined to the temple. Here monks are in a religious procession outside.

Dogen said that just to sit is to be a Buddha, thereby doing away with the duality of practice and realization: they are one and the same. Zen is notoriously cryptic, yet when people suddenly awake they often laugh out loud because enlightenment is already present, staring us right in the face.

Taisen Deshimaru once said "Zen is not a particular state but the normal state: silent, peaceful, unagitated. In Zazen neither intention, analysis, specific effort, nor imagination take place. It's enough just to be without hypocrisy, dogmatism, arrogance – embracing all opposites."

> "*Sit solidly in meditation and think not-thinking. How do you think not-thinking? Nonthinking. This is the art of Zazen.*"
>
> DOGEN

Zazen Meditation

1   Sit mindfully in the correct posture, with the resolve not to move until the end of your session.

2   You might like to sit facing the wall, as is traditional for Soto shikan-taza (intense sitting practice), or just sit in your normal place.

3   Zazen is awareness practice, so simply become aware of your thoughts and how they arise and pass.

4   Be aware of your body and what it is feeling, but do not become distracted. If you experience pain, try allowing it just to be. It may dissipate of its own accord.

5   Do not try to control or suppress thoughts, but be vigilant not to get caught up in attractive thoughts.

6   Try not to judge what arises as good or bad or neutral; just be aware of everything as it arises and passes.

7   When you notice momentary gaps between thoughts, this is pure awareness, but the minute you think this you lose it. Try to be aware without thinking.

8   Hui Neng said that being fully present is not letting the mind rest anywhere, the moment it rests thoughts arise.

9   Be aware that the mind is like a mirror, it reflects thoughts but is not the thoughts themselves.

10 When you finish your meditation, try to maintain your awareness as you move into other activities.

Left
It is simple to practice mindfulness meditation in your own home.

Koan Meditation

"*In Zen, practitioners use kung-an [koans] as subjects for meditation until their minds come to awakening. There is a big difference between a kung-an and a math problem – the solution of the math problem is included in the problem itself, while the response to the kung-an lies in the life of the practitioner.*"

THICH NHAT HANH

Koans are paradoxical riddles for which there are no conceptual answers, though they have an ultimate significance. Traditionally, students practice intensive questioning followed by an interview, or *sanzen*, with their Zen master (in Japan called a *Roshi*). The student does have to give an answer but this should reflect the ultimate question of his or her own nature, and does not make conventional "sense" of the koan.

Above
A koan (or paradoxical riddle) of the kind used traditionally in Zen teachings, which is a question without a conceptual answer or solution.

Left
The smile of this Western woman indicates that she has, perhaps, found an answer for her own personal koan through these children in Mustang, Nepal.

Koan Meditation

1 Sit in the correct posture and calm the mind for five minutes with watching or counting the breath. Remember that this is not the true purpose of meditation; it is not enough just to have a calm mind, although this is positive and beneficial.

2 We are trying to awaken to our true nature by asking a question that resonates through the core of our being: "What is this?"

3 Don't look for a conceptual answer. Keep repeating the question silently, again and again.

4 Reflect that though we could ask "Who is this?", we stay with "what," because we are shaking off our usual identity and trying to discover the mystery of what we are underneath.

5 Don't speculate intellectually, stay with the question and keep repeating it.

6 Be aware that irritation will arise – "I don't care about what this is!" – but keep asking "What is this?" and the irritation will pass.

7 If a sense of the mystery of life arises, rest in this until the mind wanders. Then return to the question.

8 Now, in this moment all there is: "What is this?"

9 When you finish your meditation, keep the question with you as you go about your life.

Right
When practicing koan meditation, speculation and the seeking of a conventional answer miss the point.

CHAPTER SIX
TIBETAN BUDDHISM

66 *There are many different philosophies, but what is of basic importance is compassion, love for others, concern for others' suffering, and reduction of selfishness. I feel that compassionate thought is the most precious thing there is. It is something that only we human beings can develop. And if we have a good heart, a warm heart, warm feelings, we will be happy and satisfied ourselves, and our friends will experience a friendly and peaceful atmosphere as well. This can be experienced nation to nation, country to country, continent to continent.* 99

THE DALAI LAMA

The Chinese Communist invasion of Tibet in 1950 was tragic news for this remote religious country, as the Communist belief that religion was "opium for the masses" led to their repression of Tibetan Buddhism. This was exacerbated by the Cultural Revolution (1966–76) and many Tibetans fled into exile in India, where they rebuilt their monasteries, and Tibetan Buddhism became accessible to the rest of the world.

Above
Rock painting, Chagpori Hill. Tibetans view the placement of prayers and sacred objects in their surroundings as an act of devotion and supplication to local deities and spirits.

Below Left
One Tibetan Buddhist meditation practice involves the making of a mandala with colored sand and its ceremonial dispersion after it is finished. Here we see a monk working on a Kalachakra mandala.

The four main schools of Tibetan Buddhism all share a basic theology based upon Mahayana philosophy. The oldest school is the Nyingma, which can be traced back to the late sixth century. Practitioners of the Nyingma tradition especially revere Padmasambhava, the great tantric master credited with introducing Buddhism into Tibet.

Nyingma

Nyingma lamas (or teachers) are sometimes married, and with less emphasis on monasticism, they are somewhat inclined to the magic of the indigenous Tibetan religion, Bon. Dzogchen – meaning great perfection – is a particular teaching of the Nyingma school. A distinctive feature of Nyingma is the *terma* tradition. These are "hidden treasures," teachings by great masters that are concealed, and meant to be discovered at a time when their wisdom will be best understood.

Sakya

The Sakya school is perhaps not as well-known today as the other traditions, though it was influential in the twelfth and thirteenth centuries. The name Sakya comes from their main monastery in south Tibet. The succession of heads of the Sakya school is hereditary, passed from uncle to nephew rather than father to son. This is unusual in Tibetan Buddhism, which usually opts for reincarnation, as with successive Dalai Lamas. The current head is the forty-first Sakya Trizin, a title taken on with the role.

Kagyu

The meaning of *Kagyu* is "transmitted command."
This school developed in the eleventh century with
the yogi Tilopa recognized as its first great master.
The Kagyus, like the Nyingmas, are also inclined to
mysticism and magic. Possibly the most well-
known of Tibetan saints is Milarepa, who was a
black magician before encountering the Buddhist
Kagyu teachings. The first Tibetan center to be
established in Europe was Samye Ling in Scotland,
which was founded by two Kagyu lamas, Chogyam
Trungpa and Akong Rinpoche.

Gelugpa

The Gelugpa school was the last to emerge in Tibet.
It was a reform movement started in the fourteenth
century by the brilliant and pious Je Tsongkhapa.
Gelug means virtuous and Je Tsongkhapa emphasized
purity and monasticism. He had studied all three of
the other schools so he aimed at creating a synthesis
of Tibetan Buddhist teachings. Teachers are almost
exclusively monks who have undertaken a study and
retreat program lasting about eighteen years, leading
to a Geshe degree. A recent offshoot from this school
is called the New Kadampa tradition.

"*Their seclusion on
the Roof of the World
enabled the Tibetans to
preserve the Mahayana
and Tantric Buddhism
of India for over a
millennium, and to
create a uniquely rich
spiritual culture.*"

JOHN SNELLING

Below
A ceremonial procession by
Tibetan monks, a custom
remaining from old Tibet when
prayers were uttered everywhere. Tibetans still recite
mantras under their breath.

How Tibetan Buddhism Is Practiced

Above

Tibetan monks are often ordained at an early age and still enjoy | playing games alongside their monastic studies.

"Erudition and philosophical rigor cultivated within a monastic context, as well as a transforming and engaged life in the world, formed the twin ideals of the early Buddhist community in Tibet."

STEPHEN BATCHELOR

P racticing Tibetan Buddhism in rebuilt monasteries in Tibet is currently permitted by the Chinese, but serious practice is discouraged. So Tibetan refugees, mainly in India, are trying to preserve their spiritual heritage in a different, modern world. Large monasteries function as study and meditation centers, and dedicated meditators still retire to caves and other isolated places for long retreats.

Many lay Tibetans are devotional, often reciting mantras as they work and go about their business. They might visit the nearby temple daily to spin prayer wheels, circumambulate, and prostrate before images of the Buddha and Tibetan saints, called *bodhisattvas*. Virtually every Tibetan is devoted to the Dalai Lama, their spiritual and temporal leader.

Tibetan Buddhism belongs to Mahayana Buddhism, so is inspired by the Bodhisattva Ideal: the wish to free all beings from suffering and confusion. The practices of Tibetan Buddhism are diverse, but all share the principle that the practitioner should receive detailed instruction and advice from a lama. A lama is a teacher or guru and a spiritual friend. Surrendering to the lama is called "Guru Devotion." By seeing buddhanature in all the lama's behavior, students are inspired to cultivate their own.

Sutra and Tantra

There are two main levels of Tibetan Buddhism: Sutra and Tantra. Practitioners start by studying the Tibetan canon of sutras and practice simple meditations to calm the mind, together with insight and visualization meditations. Students are taught the Gradual Path to Enlightenment (in Tibetan *Lam Rim*), which incorporates developing positive states of mind through practicing morality and so on, right up to enlightenment.

With Tantra we see the mystical and ritual aspects of Tibetan Buddhism. The aim is the same as any other Buddhist path – to awaken to our buddhanature – but the Tantric path, known as the quick path, appears quite different. Tantra involves using symbols of the cosmos called *mandalas* and ritual implements like bells and drums with the hands held in special postures called *mudras*. Mantras are repeated and deity practice is performed, whereby the practitioner visualizes him

Above

A mendicant monk, Lhasa, Tibet. Many Buddhist monks live by others' generosity. In return, they offer their prayers, blessings, ritual consecrations, and sometimes considerable knowledge.

Left

Tibetan Buddhist centers like this one at Samye Ling Monastery, Scotland, are springing up in the West, where increasing numbers of people are looking to the religions of the East as a way to find answers to important problems, which technology, science, and their own religions have not been able to solve.

or herself as a particular deity while reciting sacred scriptures called *sadhanas*. A deity is an embodiment of one of Buddha's qualities, such as compassion, and can be peaceful or wrathful.

Westerners are often attracted by the esoteric aspects of Tantra but it can be difficult and requires a daily commitment of reciting mantras and often an entire sadhana, complete with visualization and prayers. So it is clearly not a path for the beginner in Buddhism, though it is appropriate if undertaken after several years of preliminary practices.

Jamyang Buddhist Center Summer Retreat

"In 1983, a metropolitan Gelugpa center was established in a town house in the Finsbury Park area of London ... As the center expanded larger premises were needed, and Jamyang now occupies The Old Courthouse at Kennington, South London."

JOHN SNELLING

Above

Lama Geshe Tashi. This Tibetan teacher at the Jamyang Tibetan Buddhism Center in Kennington, London, teaches in the Gelugpa tradition of Tibetan Buddhism and leads the summer retreat.

The Jamyang Buddhist Center in London is far away from the remote meditation caves in Tibet. Yet Jamyang provides a haven of tranquility in the midst of the city, and as well as courses on Buddhism, it offers an eight-day summer retreat. The resident Tibetan teacher, Geshe Tashi, provides spiritual guidance and instruction.

The retreat runs from 8:00 am to 7:00 pm each day. People can do the whole retreat or join for one full day. The daily schedule contains a total of eight and a quarter hours' practice and starts with motivation – to awaken – and taking the eight Mahayana precepts:

1. not killing
2. not stealing
3. avoiding sexual activity
4. not lying
5. avoiding intoxicants
6. only eating one meal in 24 hours
7. not sitting on a high seat or being proud
8. not wearing adornments

A half-hour of mindfulness and calm abiding meditation is next, and there is a further session of this meditation later. After a tea break, the main practice session follows, lasting for two hours. Lam Rim (or the Gradual Path to Enlightenment) includes several subjects, such as contemplating our precious human rebirth, which are studied in turn. Another one hour of Lam Rim meditation is in the afternoon.

Vajrasattva

There is a one-hour Vajrasattva practice session. Vajrasattva is the bodhisattva of purification and the practice helps to purify our defilements and emotional

hindrances. Vajrasattva is white and holds his hands crossed at his heart – the right holding a vajra (a diamond scepter), symbolic of great bliss, and the left a bell, symbolic of the wisdom that understands emptiness. The meditation involves visualizing Vajrasattva above your head, with white light pouring from his heart on to the crown of your head, while you repeat his mantra. There is the one-hundred syllable mantra or the short mantra: "Om Vajrasattva Hum."

Finally, there are Long Life prayers, where we pray that our teachers – like the Dalai Lama – will have a long life, and Praises to the Twenty-one Taras. Tara, the Liberator, is a female bodhisattva and has twenty-one forms, all of which are ready to help us attain enlightenment. The two most common forms are White Tara, symbolic of long life, and Green Tara, who has her right leg extended ready to rise to the aid of all beings. Both White and Green Tara are said to have been born from the tears of Chenrezig. At the end of each day, any merit generated from doing these meditations is dedicated to all beings.

Above
Tibetan Buddhists often conduct ceremonies called "pujas," which include offerings of water, flowers, and food.

Below
A shrine at the Jamyang Center. This altar conveys the spiritual atmosphere at Jamyang Center.

Kagyu Samye Ling Tibetan Center

"*Not simply a monastery, not a spiritual conveyor belt, not a cultural showcase, Samye Ling is a very special place wherein are preserved some of the treasury of skills and understanding of one of the world's most extraordinary peoples – the Tibetans.*"

SAMYE LING BROCHURE

Founded in 1967, Samye Ling was the first Tibetan center to be established in the UK. There is a program of Buddhist meditation and philosophy courses, and the daily schedule for residents and visitors includes several sessions of prayers, devotional practices, and silent meditation. These periods of spiritual practice bring the community together from the various diverse activities happening throughout the center.

As well as Buddhist studies, there is a range of weekend courses including T'ai Chi, Yoga, Aromatherapy, Herbal Medicine, Shiatsu, Handwriting Analysis, Art Therapy, and other complementary therapies. These are run by qualified professionals who share an interest in, and experience of, Buddhist meditation.

Rokpa Trust is an example of compassion in action: a charity providing humanitarian aid both in the UK and abroad. Activities include regular "soup and sandwich runs" to the homeless in many cities, collecting clothes, and helping provide medicine and education for those in need around the world.

Below
Holy Island is being revived in Scotland under the direction of Tibetan Kagyu Lamas Yeshe and Akong – making real the dreams of many Western Buddhist monks, nuns, and laypeople.

birth to present and then present to pre-birth again. This allows us to see how we create our life stories.

The Tara College of Tibetan Medicine, founded in 1993, helps preserve this unique and valuable aspect of Tibetan culture. Tara College runs four-year foundation courses designed for Western students wishing to acquire the basic principles and philosophy of Tibetan medicine. Tibetan medicine takes a holistic approach to health and suffering, based on Buddhist spirituality.

Short- and long- term visitors are welcome, but accommodation must be booked in advance. Everyone is requested to keep the five precepts of not killing, not stealing, not lying, refraining from the use of intoxicants, and refraining from sexual misconduct.

Holy Island

Perhaps Samye Ling's most ambitious enterprise to date is the Holy Island Project. Holy Island lies off the west coast of Scotland and was purchased in 1991 with money from a huge and successful fund-raising initiative. Holy Island (also known as *Innis Shroin*, or "Island of the Water Spirits") has been a place of spiritual pilgrimage since the sixth-century Christian, St. Molaise, made it his home. A Center for Peace and Reconciliation is currently being built alongside a retreat center for both Buddhist and non-Buddhist meditators.

A Buddhist psychotherapy has been developed by Akong Rinpoche, cofounder of Samye Ling and Spiritual Director since 1970. Tara Rokpa Therapy is based on Buddhist philosophy, psychology, and meditation, combined with a Western psychotherapeutic understanding. A professional four-year training course is available, and the various course components, such as "Learning to Relax" and "Back to Beginnings," can also be taken as personal therapy. A major part of the course involves writing an autobiography from the present to pre-birth, pre-

The Dalai Lama

Left
This photo of the monk who was named Tenzin Gyatso, meaning "Ocean of Wisdom," aged ten, in Lhasa – before the Chinese took control of Tibet – shows a somber and studious young Dalai Lama.

Right
The Dalai Lama travels all over the world teaching the ways of peace. Behind him is a thangka of a tantric deity named Kalachakra, which literally means wheel of time.

The Dalai Lama was born in 1935 in the remote village of Takster, northeast Tibet. The fifth child of a farming family, Lhamo Thondup seemed a normal healthy boy. When he was nearly three years old, a party searching for the reincarnation of the thirteenth Dalai Lama arrived at his family's house. Tibetan custom ensured they were given tea, food, and a place to sleep for the night.

The young boy was attracted to one member of the search party and seemed to recognize his prayer beads, claiming they were his own. In fact they had belonged to the thirteenth Dalai Lama, so the search party felt he might be the boy they were seeking. They returned some weeks later with other objects belonging to the previous Dalai Lama, which Lhamo Thondup easily picked from among others. The search party realized they had finally discovered the fourteenth Dalai Lama.

He was taken to Lhasa, the capital of Tibet, and ordained and educated as befitted his new role. He was given the name of Tenzin Gyatso and formally enthroned as spiritual and political leader of Tibet. Life continued uneventfully until he was fifteen, when the Chinese invaded Tibet. He spent the next ten years trying to work with the Chinese authorities, but their systematic destruction of Buddhism and repression of the Tibetan people finally brought matters to a head, so the Dalai Lama fled to India.

Life in Exile

Today the Dalai Lama and many Tibetans still live in exile in India, in a small town called Dharamsala in the foothills of the Himalayas. The Dalai Lama is still a simple Buddhist monk and is revered and loved by his people, but he has also become world-famous as a Buddhist teacher, spokesman for peace, interfaith proponent, and international ambassador for the plight of the Tibetans. In 1989 he was awarded the Nobel Peace Prize for his valiant endeavors to resolve the Chinese occupation of Tibet without violence.

Left

Thousands gathered outside the Chinese Embassy in London in March 1999 to mark the fiftieth anniversary of Tibet's uprising against China's takeover, after which the Dalai Lama fled for his life to India. Tibet's second spiritual leader, the Panchen Lama, died in mysterious circumstances in a Chinese prison. Now his official reincarnation is missing – kidnapped by the Chinese – who chose another child to take his place. He tells Tibetans to do as "the motherland" (China) says.

"Winner of the 1989 Nobel Prize for Peace, the Dalai Lama is universally regarded as one of the great spiritual friends of our 20th century."

RICHARD GERE

Tibetan Personal View – Andrew Haynes

Above
Andrew Haynes with one of his teachers, the Tibetan monk Geshe Jampa Gyatso, who taught at a partly monastic community | in Italy where Haynes worked as Director for some years. There he met his wife, with whom he moved to London.

I grew up in the Caribbean and Britain with many different cultures and religions, and in 1979 I came to London to be a student. I encountered ideas of every political hue and found life exciting but hectic. The culture was materialistic, and even those who reacted against it had little ethical basis for their actions.

I wanted a spiritual direction and started meditating every day, soon realizing it was the most important thing in my life. My first retreat lasted ten days, and I experienced a part of my being that I had never previously touched. I became a Buddhist despite having little knowledge of Buddhist philosophy.

After university I determined to dedicate my life to Buddhism through work, study, and choice of living companions, but soon realized I needed to move on from the group that had introduced me to Buddhism. I then met Serkong Rinpoche, a Tibetan lama born and educated in Tibet. He had been a junior tutor to the Dalai Lama but had fled into exile after the Chinese invasion. I knew I had made direct contact with an ancient, pure, and vital spiritual tradition.

In 1982 I saw a photograph of Lama Thubten Yeshe and instantly determined to meet him, so I flew to Italy to attend a course with him. His energy and enthusiasm were infectious, and everyone knew we were sharing a rare and precious opportunity. The Italians had an emotional rather than an intellectual approach to Buddhism, which suited me. I was quite intellectual but had felt the emotional limitations of being a young man in Britain in the early '80s. Tibetan Buddhism was comprehensive enough to deal with my intellectual, emotional, and spiritual needs.

In autumn 1983 I moved to a Buddhist center in the Italian countryside, which became my home for the next six years. The resident teacher, Geshe Jampa Gyatso, taught us from the

syllabus of the Tibetan monastic universities. He was an ordained monk, as were some of the Western students, and it was very inspirational to live in a partly monastic community.

Becoming Director

In 1986 I became Director of the center, which had about thirty residents and up to a hundred and fifty visitors at any time. This left little space for my own selfish needs and wants, and I was forced to become more aware of others and how to look after them! The job was very satisfying but demanding, and after three years I decided to leave while I still felt positive about the experience.

Above
Lama Zong Rinpoche. *Lama* is an honorific title given to Tibetan Buddhist monks and means teacher. Zong Rinpoche taught both Tibetans and Westerners in India until his death in 1984.

Left
The Institute of Lama Tzongkhapa in Pomaia, Italy, where Tibetan Buddhism is taught to Westerners by Tibetan lamas and monks, who expect Buddhism to change once it is established in the West. Change being an inevitable part of life, according to their view as Buddhists, they do not resist it as much as Western religious leaders often do.

In 1987 I met my future wife, Teresa, who was visiting the center for the summer. I returned to London in 1989 and she followed me in 1991. Although her spiritual practice is not focused on one religion, Buddhism has made a tremendous contribution to our relationship, which I find most harmonious.

In London I have worked in local government administration and, more recently, information systems, also helping to manage a Buddhist center, which has been very rewarding. I have taught meditation and Buddhist philosophy, a direct way of sharing the benefits I have gained personally. Buddhism has given a direction to my life and in this way has helped me to be a happier, more positive person.

Tibetan Prayers

Above
Here the Dalai Lama is studying a traditional Tibetan Buddhist text. Prayers and study of texts together give a balanced approach to Buddhism.

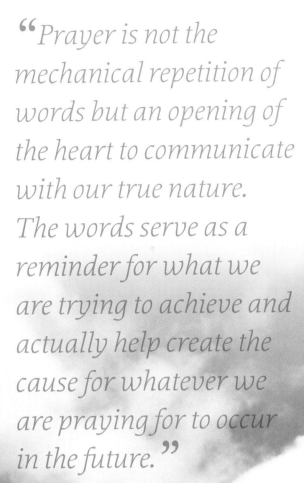

"Prayer is not the mechanical repetition of words but an opening of the heart to communicate with our true nature. The words serve as a reminder for what we are trying to achieve and actually help create the cause for whatever we are praying for to occur in the future."

KATHLEEN MCDONALD

THE PRAYER OF REFUGE

The Prayer of Refuge can be repeated three times, in Tibetan or English, according to preference, at the beginning of a meditation session:

Sang. gyay. cho.dang tsog.kyi chog. nam.la
Jang. chub bar. du dag.ni kyab. su.chi
Dag.gi jin.sog gyi.pay so.nam.gyi
Dro.la pen.chir sang.gyay drub.par.shog

I take refuge until I am enlightened
in the buddhas, the dharma, and the sangha.
Through the merit I create by practicing giving and
the other perfections
May I attain buddhahood for the sake of all
sentient beings.

THE DALAI LAMA'S PRAYER

The Dalai Lama has a favorite short prayer that gives him "great inspiration and determination." This can be silently repeated at any time, to remind ourselves why we are practicing Buddhism:

For as long as space endures,
And for as long as living beings remain,
Until then may I, too, abide
To dispel the misery of the world.

DEDICATION OF MERIT AND BODHICITTA

The Dedication of Merit and the Bodhicitta Prayer can be said, in Tibetan or English, once each at the end of a meditation session:

Ge.wa di.yi nyur.du.dag
La.ma sang.gyay drub.gyur.nay
Dro.wa chig.kyang ma.lu.pa
De.yi sa.la go.par.shog

Through this virtuous action
May I quickly attain the state of a guru-Buddha
And lead every living being, without exception,
Into that pure world.

Jang.chub sem.chog rin.po.che
Ma.kye pa.nam kye.gyur.chig
Kye.pa nyam.pa may.pa.yi
Gong.nay gong.du pel.war.shog

May the supreme jewel bodhicitta
That has not arisen, arise and grow;
And may that which has arisen not diminish
But increase more and more.

DROMTON RINPOCHE

One day a great lama, Dromton Rinpoche, was giving teachings in a place near Lhasa, the capital of Tibet. During a break he went for a walk in the woods nearby and saw a man conscientiously circumambulating a stupa, a shrine symbolizing Buddha's inner qualities. Circumambulating stupas, or other Buddhist shrines, is a traditional Buddhist practice to accumulate merit.

The man asked Rinpoche if this was the correct way to perform circumambulations. Rinpoche smiled and replied, "I rejoice in your actions, but I wish you would practice pure Dharma." The man was a little puzzled, but then thought, "Perhaps this is not the best practice, I had better try doing prostrations."

The next day during his walk Rinpoche came across the same man prostrating in front of a statue of the Buddha at the temple. The man was pleased to see the great teacher again, greeted him reverentially, and anxiously asked if he was prostrating correctly. Rinpoche smiled and answered, "What you are doing is very good, but it would be even better if you tried to practice pure Dharma."

The man felt confused and once again thought he was doing the wrong practice. So he reflected, "If prostrating is not the correct practice, maybe I should start reciting mantras." So he sat down in the temple and started to recite a particular mantra. The next day Rinpoche passed by the temple and heard the man earnestly reciting the mantra. When the man saw Rinpoche he thought "This time I must have got it right," and said to Dromton Rinpoche, "Now I am practicing pure Dharma."

Rinpoche smiled compassionately at the man, then folded his hands together and replied: "I really appreciate your recitation of this mantra, but pure Dharma has to do with motivation. If your mind is still dominated by the desire for selfish material gain and fame, then whatever practice you choose to do cannot be the pure practice of Dharma. Please try to overcome this first by being aware of impermanence and death. Once you have attained a realization of death and impermanence, then all the practices you do will be pure Dharma."

The man listened carefully to Rinpoche's teaching and took his advice to heart. He realized that his motivation had not been pure while he was circumambulating, prostrating, and reciting mantras. So this time he started to meditate with single-pointed concentration on death and impermanence and soon was able to achieve many high realizations without too much effort.

The Proper Motivation

This story is a good reminder to develop proper motivation before we start whichever Dharma practice we are thinking of doing. It is only too easy to fool ourselves in our Buddhist practice by thinking such things as: "If I generate a lot of good karma through this practice, then I might be rewarded with getting things that I want." As we can see from the story, accumulating merit is not sufficient to lead us toward enlightenment.

Unless we are constantly aware of death and impermanence we can easily be tempted by the desire for fame, even if this is just wanting people to think well of us, and for material gain, even if we think that extra wealth will give us more time for Buddhist practice. Both of these desires contain a subtly selfish, impure motivation.

But if, like the man in the story, we meditate on death and impermanence first, our motivation will become pure. With this awareness we can really overcome the unhappiness and dissatisfaction caused by desire and attachment.

Below
Dromton Rinpoche was able to teach his disciple that true Dharma comes from pure motivation. An awareness of impermanence and death helps purify motivation.

Meditation on the Clarity of the Mind

Above
This Tibetan nun studies in a relaxed Western manner beside a large dog – which she might have avoided in her country!

"*Meditation is not a matter of trying to achieve ecstasy, spiritual bliss, or tranquility; nor is it attempting to become a better person. It is simply the creation of a space in which we are able to expose and undo our neurotic games, our self-deceptions, our hidden hopes and fear.*"

CHOGYAM TRUNGPA

Left
A Nepalese statue of Vajrasattva holding a vajra in the right hand, symbolizing skillful means, and a bell in the left hand, symbolizing wisdom. The tantric practice of Vajrasattva is used for purification.

Meditation on the Clarity of Mind

By meditating on the clarity of our mind we can experience the clear and transient nature of our thoughts and feelings. In this way we lessen our self-identification with them. This is especially useful if we have low self-esteem – which is based on believing our thoughts and feelings about ourselves – as we can experience them simply arising and passing on to other thoughts and feelings.

1   Start with a simple breathing meditation for a few minutes to let go of thoughts.

2   Once the mind is calm, turn your attention to your consciousness, or mind. Your mind is whatever you are experiencing at this moment. Whether your thoughts, feelings, and sensations are troubled or happy, their nature is pure and clear like space. There is no form, shape, or color, just awareness.

3   This is probably difficult when we start, as we confuse the content of our thoughts with their nature. If this is your experience, then you can do the following visualization. Imagine lying on your back in a tranquil rural meadow. Look up at the sky and all you see is vast, clear space. Concentrate on this open spaciousness and imagine you become one with it. Reflect that this is the true nature of your mind and all that manifests in it. When you become distracted by a thought or feeling, remind yourself of its pure, clear nature and return to the open spaciousness.

4   Don't try to reflect on what the mind is, simply experience its pure nature.

5   At the end of your meditation session, dedicate any merit created for the benefit of all beings.

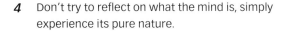

Right
To experience clarity of mind, it may be helpful to use a suitable visualization to achieve this state.

Meditation on Death

Above
Children are treated with care and respect by Buddhists, who treat all sentient beings as if they were once their mother. Reincarnation as a human being is considered to be very precious.

Below
Tibetan monk lighting butter lamps, perhaps meditating on impermanence and death.

" *Although today I am healthy, Well-nourished and unafflicted, Life is momentary and deceptive: The body is like an object on loan for but a minute.* "

SHANTIDEVA

Meditation on Death

Meditating on death helps us work out which attitudes and activities are really precious. The shock of contemplating our own death is short-lived, because it is inescapable. Then – ironically – we do not feel morbid but learn to appreciate our life. Death meditation is a good antidote to boredom.

Traditionally, death meditation has nine points, which are divided into three sections:

Inevitability of death

1   Everyone will die, including you.

2   In the time it takes to read this sentence you are nearer to death; life flows on and cannot be stopped.

3   Assess how you spend your life and how much time you spend on activities like meditating, which are beneficial. How much time do you spend doing things that will seem pointless when you die?

Uncertainty of time of death

4   Life can end at any time – in an accident, perhaps. You cannot know when you will die, so make the most of each moment.

5   There are many causes of death, from violence to poison. You don't know if you might encounter any of these.

6   Our bodies are fragile and prone to illness; even if you feel well now, this may not last.

Only spiritual insight is useful when you die

7   Possessions cannot be taken with us, so are of no use when we die.

8   Friends and family can do nothing when we die, death can be experienced only alone.

9   Even our own bodies cannot be relied upon, they become useless when we die.

Right
Don't get depressed about death! It is as natural as birth, and they are both a part of living.

Meditation on Compassion

"*By gradually developing our mind, our present limited compassion will grow and expand to become great compassion. This is made possible by reflecting again and again on the suffering of others...*"

GESHE RABTEN

Left
Padmapani Avalokiteshvara, also known as Chenrezig in Tibet, is the bodhisattva of compassion. His female counterpart is Tara, who corresponds to Kwan Yin in Chinese Buddhism. The Dalai Lama is said to be the embodiment of Chenrezig.

Meditation on Compassion

Compassion is the desire to free others from suffering. This does not mean feeling sad but is the understanding of how suffering occurs and how we can be helpful. Nor do we become a world savior, thinking we can help everyone. We must learn our limits – when we can help and when not. Meditating on Avalokiteshvara, the embodiment of the Buddha's compassion, awakens our potential for compassion.

1 Calm the mind with breathing meditation.

2 Think about the suffering experienced by beings everywhere.

3 Develop the aspiration to open your heart and help beings be free of suffering.

4 Reflect that the causes of suffering are confused mental and emotional states arising from misperceiving how things really are.

5 Contemplate that this is why you too experience suffering, and feel compassion toward yourself.

6 Visualize Avalokiteshvara above your head. He has a translucent white body and smiles, radiating compassion for all beings. He has four arms: the first two hold a wish-fulfilling jewel at his heart; of the second pair, the right holds a crystal rosary, the left a white lotus. He sits in the full lotus posture.

7 Generate the wish to develop compassion and request Avalokiteshvara to hear your prayer.

8 In response, streams of white light pour from his heart into you, purifying your negativities and filling you with love, compassion, and peace. The white light then streams out and touches all beings.

9 While maintaining the visualization, recite Avalokiteshvara's mantra, "Om Mani Padme Hum," aloud or quietly. The sacred syllables resonate with our potential enlightened qualities. Do this for as long as you wish.

10 Avalokiteshvara dissolves into white light which flows into your heart. Your mind merges with his and you feel tranquil and blissful.

11 Hold the visualization and if your mind wanders, gently bring it back to Avalokiteshvara.

12 Finally, dedicate any merit to the happiness of all beings.

Below
Our compassion can be awakened by meditating on Avalokiteshvara – the embodiment of Buddha's compassion.

ajahn: honorary title for a senior bhikkhu, or abbot

bhikkhu: a monk in the Theravada tradition

bodhicitta: the altruistic mind that aspires to attain enlightenment in order to help all beings find happiness

bodhisattva: someone on the path to enlightenment who has generated bodhicitta

Buddha: an enlightened being; the first of the Three Jewels

Buddha Shakyamuni: the historical Buddha, Siddartha Gautama

Buddhadharma: literally the teachings of the Buddha

buddhanature: the inherent potential in all beings to become a Buddha

compassion: the wish to free all beings from suffering

conventional, also relative, truth: the way things appear to those who are not yet enlightened and unable to perceive ultimate truth

deity: a Buddha represented in a symbolic form, peaceful or wrathful

deity practice: a form of Tibetan tantric practice using meditation, mantra, and visualization on a particular deity

Dharma or Dhamma: can mean several things, but here it is used to mean the word of the Buddha, the Buddha's teachings; the second of the Three Jewels

dokusan: interview with a Zen teacher, or roshi

Gelugpa: one of the four main schools of Tibetan Buddhism

geshe: an honorary title for a monk in the Gelugpa tradition of Tibetan Buddhism

gompa: Tibetan meditation hall

guru: spiritual teacher or master

Hinayana: literally – but somewhat misleadingly – lesser vehicle. The path followed by Buddhist traditions that try to realize enlightenment for the individual, but also the basis for Mahayana Buddhism

karma: the actions of our body, speech, and mind. Whether good or bad, they are motivated by unenlightened delusion and serve as the cause for future rebirth – good actions cause good rebirth, and vice versa. But karma operates over many lifetimes and conditions must be appropriate for karma to ripen, thus it is more complex than simple cause and effect

Kagyu: one of the four main schools of Tibetan Buddhism

koan: enigmatic Zen phrase used as a meditation practice

lama: Tibetan spiritual teacher or guru

Mahayana: literally, greater vehicle; the Buddhist path that tries to realize enlightenment for the benefit of all beings

mantra: sacred syllables, usually repeated many times as part of spiritual practice

meditation: there are two principal types: analytical and single-pointed concentration. Both train the mind and work toward transformation of consciousness

Nirvana or Nibbana: literally, liberation from samsara (or cyclic existence)

Nyingma: one of the four main schools of Tibetan Buddhism

reincarnation: the most subtle level of consciousness, together with the karma accrued by the previous incarnations that passes from one lifetime to the next

Rinzai: one of the two main traditions of Japanese Zen, founded by Eisai

roshi: Japanese Zen master or teacher

sadhana: a Tibetan religious text detailing a tantric practice and

including instructions on saying mantras, visualization, and recitation of prayers and praises

Sakya: one of the four main schools of Tibetan Buddhism

samatha: tranquil abiding or calm meditation

samsara: literally, cyclic existence; continuously being born and dying and being reborn again before a person achieves enlightenment and enters Nirvana

Sangha: the spiritual community, our spiritual friends; sometimes used to mean monks and nuns only – the third of the Three Jewels

satipatthana: mindful awareness meditation

shikan-taza: intensive sitting meditation in the Soto tradition of Zen

Soto: one of the two main traditions of Japanese Zen, founded by Dogen

sunyata: literally, emptiness or voidness; a philosophy believing all things are empty of inherent existence, i.e. they cannot exist alone but depend upon their constituent parts and environment

sutra or sutta: the teachings of the Buddha, spoken or written

tantra or tantrayana: also called vajrayana in the Tibetan tradition. Literally, continuity; usually meaning deity practice which aims to transform a person's body, speech, and mind into a Buddha

Three Jewels: Buddha, Dharma, and Sangha: all a person needs to rely on, or take refuge in, to reach enlightenment

ultimate truth: the way things really are, i.e. empty of inherent existence and interdependent on their constituent parts and environment

vipassana: insight meditation

zazen: sitting meditation in the Zen tradition

Aitken, Robert, *The Practice of Perfection*, Washington, Counterpoint, 1997

Batchelor, Martine, *Principles of Zen*, London, Thorsons, 1999

Batchelor, Martine, *Walking on Lotus Flowers*, London, Thorsons, 1996

Batchelor, Stephen, *Buddhism Without Beliefs*, New York, Riverhead Books, 1997

Batchelor, Stephen, *The Awakening of the West*, London, Aquarian, 1994

Batchelor, Stephen, *The Faith to Doubt*, California, Parallax Press, 1990

Beer, Robert, *The Encyclopedia of Tibetan Symbols and Motifs*, London, Serindia Publications, 1999

Bodhi, Bhikkhu, *The Noble Eightfold Path*, Kandy, Buddhist Publication Society, 1994

Chah, Ajahn, *Bodhinyana*, Thailand, Bung Wai Forest Monastery, 1980

Dalai Lama, *Kindness, Clarity, and Insight*, New York, Snow Lion Publications, 1985

Dalai Lama, *The Meaning of Life from a Buddhist Perspective*, Boston, Wisdom Publications, 1992

Dogen, *Moon in a Dewdrop*, Shaftesbury, Element Books, 1988

Farrer-Halls, Gill, *The World of the Dalai Lama*, London, Thorsons, 1998

Hanh, Thich Nhat, *Zen Keys*, London, Thorsons, 1995

Kapleau, Roshi Philip, *The Three Pillars of Zen*, New York, Anchor Books, 1989

McDonald, Kathleen, *How to Meditate*, Boston, Wisdom Publications, 1984

Morreale, Don (ed.), *The Complete Guide to Buddhist America*, Boston, Shambhala, 1998

Narada Thera (trans.), *The Dhammapada*, London, John Murray, 1959

Rabten, Geshe Tamdin, *Treasury of Dharma*, London, Tharpa Publications, 1988

Sasaki, Ruth F., *The Record of Lin-Chi*, Kyoto, The Institute for Zen Studies, 1975

Shantideva, *A Guide to the Bodhisattva's Way of Life*, Dharamsala, Library of Tibetan Works and Archives, 1992

Snelling, John, *The Buddhist Handbook*, London, Rider, 1997

Snelling, John, *The Elements of Buddhism*, Shaftesbury, Element Books, 1990

Sumedho, Ajahn, *Mindfulness: The Path to the Deathless*, Hemel Hempstead, Amaravati Publications, 1987

Sunim, Kusan, *The Way of Korean Zen*, New York, Weatherhill, 1985

Trungpa, Chogyam, *The Myth of Freedom*, Boulder & London, Shambhala, 1976

Wangchen, Geshe Namgyal, *Awakening the Mind of Enlightenment*, London, Wisdom Publications, 1987

Wright, Arthur F., *Buddhism in Chinese History*, California, Stanford University Press, 1982

Yampolsky, Philip B. (trans.), *The Platform Sutra of the Sixth Patriarch*, New York, Colombia University Press, 1967

Yampolsky, Philip B., *The Zen Master Hakuin*, New York, Columbia University Press, 1971